LAST CHANCE

PRESERVING LIFE ON EARTH

Larry J. Schweiger

President and CEO of the National Wildlife Federation

FULCRUM

GOLDEN, COLORADO

Library of Congress Cataloging-in-Publication Data

Schweiger, Larry J.
 Last chance : preserving life on earth / Larry J. Schweiger.
     p. cm.
 Includes bibliographical references and index.
 ISBN 978-1-55591-717-3 (hardcover)
 1. Global warming. 2. Global environmental change. 3. Greenhouse effect, Atmospheric. 4. Plants--Effect of global warming on. 5. Glaciers--Environmental aspects. 6. Polar bear--Effect of pollution on. 7. Environmental protection. 8. Conservation of natural resources. I. Title.
 QC981.9.G56S38 2009
 363.738'74--dc22

                         2009014560

This book was printed using low-VOC inks on 100 percent recycled paper in the United States by Thomson-Shore, Inc. The jacket and case materials also contain recycled content. Thomson-Shore is a member of the Green Press Initiative and is certified by the Forest Stewardship Council.

0 9 8 7 6 5 4 3 2 1

Fulcrum Publishing
4690 Table Mountain Dr., Ste. 100
Golden, CO 80403
800-992-2908 • 303-277-1623
www.fulcrumbooks.com

This book is dedicated to my entire family, especially my wife, Clara, who has patiently supported me through long hours and many weeks on the road, and to my daughters, Della, Carolyn, and Lauren, and their families, with the hope that the world finds the moral courage to stop polluting the air to protect the future for Thaddy, Patrick, and their entire generation. This is also a tribute to my parents, George and Margaret, who raised me to love the out-of-doors, and to my grandmother, Carolyn Malseed, who inspired me with her love and wisdom.

Contents

FOREWORD

From time to time our nation has had to face great crises that required us to acknowledge difficult truths in order to make necessary change. Each crisis was predicted by prophets who were able to see with clarity the need for change. Initially, the prophets were at best ignored, but more often they were reviled by segments of the population. Yet, after making the change, the nation has always emerged stronger. Change is unsettling, and its prospect almost always engenders tremendous resistance.

In the decades leading up to the Civil War, the abolitionists were the prophets who aroused a ferocious opposition in both the North and the South. However, they saw more clearly than most what Abraham Lincoln so brilliantly articulated in the Lincoln-Douglas debates: "A house divided against itself cannot stand. I believe this government cannot endure permanently half slave and half free." Despite the horrendous cost of the Civil War, the nation ultimately emerged stronger as a result.

Scarcely a decade after the end of the Civil War, another group of prophets emerged: hunters, fishermen, artists, and natural historians who began to cry out against the unrestrained exploitation of the nation's natural resources, which, unless checked, would soon result in the destruction of our forests, wilderness, and wildlife. These prophets engendered strong opposition from timber, mining, and railroad interests. Yet, they had considerable success. The designation of Yellowstone National Park in 1872 as the first national park in any country marked the tenuous beginning of what ultimately became an extraordinary burst of conservation in which millions of acres of national forests were protected and national parks and wildlife refuges were established.

While most Americans are aware of the history of the conservation movement, few are aware of the immensely important role played by hunters, fishermen, and artists. Spending time in the outdoors, they saw firsthand what was happening to the continent's wildlife, woods, and prairies. They spoke up and provided critical leadership in order to leave future generations an extraordinary heritage that we have a responsibility to pass on to our children's children. We owe a great debt to artists such as Albert Bierstadt and Thomas Moran, whose paintings of western landscapes were so stunning that initially many observers thought the landscapes were figments of the artists' imagination. They helped the public and Congress "see" the beauty and majesty of the western lands.

George Bird Grinnell, who is virtually unknown today, was a leader in helping the nation develop policies so that Yellowstone National Park could become a park for all of the nation's people and not government land to be plundered by the railroads, mining and timber companies, and poachers. Indeed, when Yellowstone was established as a national park, there were no laws or enforcement mechanisms to protect the resource. As a young man, Grinnell had hunted bison with a group of Pawnee. This experience and his extensive travels through the American West allowed him to see with more clarity than almost anyone else that unless effective laws were enacted, the bison faced extinction, including the few that still survived in Yellowstone National Park. As editor of *Forest and Stream* for more than two decades, with enormous determination and skill, Grinnell led the fight to pass legislation to provide for effective protection of Yellowstone National Park. Several times they came perilously close to losing as Congress attempted to break up the park in order to build a railroad. Grinnell called his opponents "conscienceless money-hunters in the US Congress." Finally, the fortuitous capture of a notorious poacher at a time when a writer from *Forest and Stream* and a well-respected photographer were present to document the poacher's gruesome handiwork set off a political firestorm that resulted in the passage of the Lacey Act, which provided the desperately needed protection for Yellowstone National Park.

Larry Schweiger is another such leader, a contemporary prophet. As an outdoorsman, hunter, and fisherman, he has seen firsthand the damage done to our western forests by the pine beetles no longer kept in check by cold winters. Thousands and thousands of acres of timberlands have been killed by these beetles. He has seen what the melting of the Arctic ice sheet has done to the polar bear's habitat. He has traveled to Greenland to see the impact of warmer temperatures on that island's ice sheet. He documents the changes in bird migratory patterns resulting from climate change. He has carefully and thoughtfully read scientific journals and papers and explains how small changes in temperature are resulting in dangerous temperature amplifications that are accelerating the rate of climate change. Most importantly, he feels a strong moral obligation to act as a steward for our planet and has written a compelling book on the necessary policy measures to mitigate the impacts of climate change. Thoughtfully, he challenges each of us to take the time to become familiar with the science of climate change and then to act as responsible citizens to change our behavior and to hold our elected officials responsible for enacting farsighted policies to address climate change.

—Theodore Roosevelt IV

PREFACE

I have long been troubled by the mounting scientific evidence pointing to the unprecedented ecological and societal threats presented by global warming. Nineteen ecological scientists studying six representative ecoregions covering 20 percent of the earth's land area concluded that unless we cut greenhouse gas emissions significantly, somewhere between 15 and 37 percent of all living resources of this planet could become extinct or on the road to extinction by 2050.[1] That warning hit home for me, as I have spent my life trying to keep wildlife in our future. Recent findings from the Intergovernmental Panel on Climate Change are even more dire.[2]

I suffer no illusions about the magnitude of the difficulties ahead. "Fight no little battles," my childhood mentor, Ralph Abele, often challenged. As a company commander in the Third Armored Division of the US Army, Ralph served in five campaigns in the European theater, including the dreadful Normandy invasion, where he fought stubbornly. As the sole survivor from his landing craft, Ralph knew the cost of stubborn courage. His gravelly voice, long silenced by death, still speaks clearly to me as I write this book. Drawing from many published science reports and presenting the subject in language we can all understand, I hope to reach enough people who care to make a difference in this, the greatest battle in the history of wildlife conservation.

Unborn children do not have a vote in the matter if we do not vote for them. They have no way to take action apart from our actions. Our oldest daughter, Della, has two little boys, and our middle daughter, Carolyn, is pregnant with our third grandchild. Unless we act right now, they will witness a global catastrophe unprecedented in human history. How great a debt will we owe them if we fail to act now? We must quickly transition from fossil fuels to a more secure, efficient, and renewable energy future that draws on clean energy and creates millions of green-collar jobs. We can invest energy dollars at home while protecting the nature of tomorrow. Looking ahead, I cling to the hope that Americans will cut through all of the cynical obfuscation and discover the truth about what lies ahead for all humanity. For the sake of all children, please join with me in this effort to avoid a climate crisis and keep wildlife alive and thriving.

ACKNOWLEDGMENTS

I first became active in wildlife conservation as a volunteer when I was fourteen. Since that day forty-five years ago, I have been blessed by wise mentors and dedicated and supportive colleagues who have made a difference in the world and in my life. I have worked with many unselfish volunteers affiliated with the National Wildlife Federation who gave their time and money to defend the future for wildlife. I am privileged to work with some of the finest conservationists. We have a dedicated board of directors, a president's advisory council, a dedicated staff, and more than 4 million generous members, donors, volunteers, and affiliate leaders who love wildlife. I also am thankful for the many environmental, conservation, sportsmen, and faith groups that work with us every day to solve the problem of this pressing danger.

I want to especially acknowledge the thoughtful input and feedback of several colleagues, including Kara Ball, Jennifer Jones, and Julie Lalo. Doug Inkley and Amanda Staudt provided very helpful science review. Individual chapters were also reviewed by Michael Murray, Julie Sibbing, Kevin Coyle, Kurt Zwally, Steve Torbit, and John Kostyack, who were each generous with their contributions. Amanda

Cooke reviewed the citations and offered other helpful suggestions. A special thanks to Jaime Matyas, Jeremy Symons, and to Jackie Hardy, my senior executive assistant, who among other duties manages my schedule so that I could squeeze in time to write. I also wish to thank the staff of Fulcrum Publishing for all their guidance and help getting this publication into print.

Introduction

THE NATURE OF TOMORROW

We are truly heirs of all the ages; but as honest men it behooves us to learn the extent of our inheritance, and as brave ones not to whimper if it should prove less than we had supposed.

—John Tyndall, 1890

Look forward with me to the year 2020. What kind of world do you hope to find ten years from now? Will healthy, diverse ecosystems with complete assemblages of fish, wildlife, plants, and trees continue? Will we maintain productive farm soils and verdant forestlands? Will our towns and cities be livable and sustainable? What will become of those wild rivers and streams where we canoe and fish, the remote forests where we hike, bird-watch, or hunt? What will happen to those extravagant alpine wildflower meadows, lush forest landscapes, and broad sweeps of sagebrush that the American West is best known for? What will become of coastal marshes, sand beaches, and coral reefs? What is to become of the nature of tomorrow?

Our ancestors polluted a lot of air and water, burned through vast virgin forests, destroyed enormous bison herds, and permanently altered some of the most fertile soils on the planet long before our generation inherited this world. However, on our watch the pace of ecological destruction and global warming has accelerated through the latter half of the twentieth century as populations soared and developing nations emulated the Western world with their energy and resource usage. With the current pace of climate change, it is hard to imagine what life will look like even ten years from now.

Beyond the worst-case predictions made even a few years ago, climate change is now occurring more rapidly in the twenty-first century. As recently as 2004, scientists were concerned that Arctic sea ice could melt within the century.[1] Now some National Aeronautics and Space Administration scientists are predicting that this may happen by 2012.[2] This forecast was lent weight by a dramatic, record-shattering low point in Arctic sea ice in the summer of 2007.

It is now becoming clear that the earth's energy balance is much more fragile than we previously believed. If summer Arctic ice disappears in a few short years and the tundra heats up and releases large quantities of methane, more climate and ecological change may occur in ten to twenty years than occurred in the past one thousand years. Unchecked, the planet is heading to a full-blown climate crisis as it encounters several key tipping points triggered by rapid Arctic warming. Former vice president Al Gore recently warned a gathering of faith leaders in Nashville, Tennessee, that global warming now has the capacity to "disrupt the context for human civilization."[3]

Like it or not, global warming is the defining issue of the twenty-first century, and this may be the defining moment for an all-out effort to avoid a climate crisis. Many who are paying attention to what is going on perceive the enormous risks ahead, but there are too many who are not paying attention.[4] For decades, we have been watching pollution accumulate in the atmosphere, building ever rapidly to a day of reckoning. Once the planet passes certain climatic tipping points, there is little or no room for going back. We are living through a nightmare that only gets deeper and darker each day as humanity continues to ignore the warnings and fails to address what is happening to the earth's atmosphere.

Those who say that global warming will destroy the earth are wrong. The overheated earth will survive and continue to spin through space for millions of years to come. It is life on earth as we have known it that is at stake. In the lifetime of a child born today, according to the Intergovernmental Panel on Climate Change, some 20 to 30 percent of the world's plant and animal species will likely be on the brink of extinction from global warming, even if we take action right now. Even more foreboding, 40 to 70 percent of all species could be extinct within our children's lifetimes if we don't take action now.[5] Are we ready to tell our children that much of what we have enjoyed on earth will not be available to them? Are we ready to face the verdict that our neglect has harmed the ones we love most?

This is not a book written by a scientist attempting to document the many climate threats. There are more than enough outstanding scientific publications detailing global warming, and they are backed up by more than ten thousand scientific studies. I reference a few of them here, in hopes that my words will help theirs find more ears.

While I include a chapter on new energy opportunities, this is not a search for alternative energy technologies, either.

We have enough existing technology to deploy—including advanced wind turbines in our windy landscapes, huge solar-thermal power plants for the desert Southwest, and large-scale geothermal units suitable for many regions of the country—to provide for daily electrical needs. Photovoltaics, geothermal, and, most importantly, energy efficiency in our homes as well as civic and commercial buildings can eventually eliminate the need for fossil fuel usage in the building sector. Energy from tidal flows, wave action, and river currents can provide some additional energy and needed stability to the electric grid. Electric cars and high-speed, sustainable transportation systems can cut ground transportation fossil fuel usage by more than 80 percent over the next decade or so. By then, we will have enough new technology to end all carbon emissions. In the meantime, we must accelerate the recapturing of atmospheric carbon in soils and forests by assisting farmers and other landowners to change their practices in order to capture more carbon.

Nor is this book about economics, although solving the climate crisis will strengthen our still-dark economic future as we keep money spent on energy production at home. Standard economic tools, including economic discount curves, don't work in situations such as global warming that will cause catastrophic losses in the future if unaddressed now. Valuations of future benefits must be about intergenerational justice and moral obligations to our children rather than about traditional investment analysis and decision making. If foreign invaders were assembling forces near our shores, we would not be using economic calculations to decide whether we should spend money to get ready for battle. This is that kind of moment.

Seeing the stark alternatives, I struggled writing this book. On one hand, I can imagine millions awakening from a long interlude of indifference and denial to scientific reality as they discover vast stores of published scientific research illuminating the climate dangers. On the other hand, because the cause and effect are separated by time, I can see global warming continuing like a thief in the night in stealthlike form, until it is too late to do anything about it. These two scenarios have long haunted me, as they remain in a deadly struggle for dominance. My hope is that by seeing the urgency of the threats before us, Americans will turn the political wheel in time to avoid the horrific crash.

If we do, our victory will be a triumph of one way of life over another. It will be a moral victory proving that we have the discipline to give up selfish behaviors to care for our children and their world, a victory for the rights of unborn generations and a victory restoring the integrity of all forms of life on earth. It will also be a victory for human dignity, earned through the integrity of choosing a higher purpose over the squanderer's reckless consumption.

I believe in transparency of motives. This book is a call from an outdoorsperson who harbors respect for science, a Christian perspective, and a lifelong love for this gift we call nature. I believe that each of us has a moral and stewardship obligation for nature regardless of our faith, politics, or worldview. Surely we can agree that wrecking the planet is an ethical abomination.

I am a registered political independent. I judge politicians on what they actually do, not by their party affiliation. Having spent forty years advocating for wildlife in various legislative venues, I believe in the power of volunteers working together to change the future. I write therefore to those who share this love, to inform, encourage, and foster bold actions by millions to restore balance to the world's climate system and to protect nature for tomorrow.

Global warming has been misbranded as purely an environmental threat; on the contrary, it is also a societal threat affecting everyone on the planet. We have both a personal and a societal responsibility to care for our children's future. While there are important things we can do as individuals, solving the climate crisis requires societal-scale responses and actions. This job is too big to leave for a few environmentalists in Washington, DC.

We must all do our part. I am reminded of something that Civil War hero and founder of the Red Cross, Clara Barton, once said about her motivation to go onto active battlefields to rescue wounded soldiers. (She was not trained as a nurse but did not use that as an excuse.) Volunteering in fearful conditions, Clara simply rejected "the folly and wickedness of remaining quietly at home."[6] Clara's courageous action inspired thousands of other women to donate medical supplies and to volunteer in various ways to support the wounded troops.

At this moment, with a new administration in place, the United States is finally poised to take steps to address global warming. My remaining fear is that vested interests will thwart or shorten our steps so that, in the end, our steps will not be big enough. We cannot take baby steps when much bolder action is required. Wholesale transformation of our energy economy will only happen if it is triggered by grassroots voices demanding bold legislative and executive actions in Washington, DC, and in every state and territory.

After all, in this democracy, voters are the sovereign authority. If our government stinks, it is because we collectively stink. When it comes to nature, there are two kinds of people in our world today: those who care and those who do not. You can tell them apart not just by their words, but by their actions. I write to those who care. Be a person who cares and show it by acting in concert with others who care.

I am reminded of the story of Balaam riding his ass in Mesopotamia. Recorded in the book of Numbers, God warns Balaam not to travel to a certain dangerous place. Balaam stiffens his neck, ignores the warning, and goes on a perverse journey down the wrong path leading to a very dangerous place. Along the way, Balaam's ass sees an angel that is not visible to Balaam, senses the impending disaster, and tries to warn Balaam. After three failed attempts, the ass finally sits down and starts talking. Shocked by a talking ass, Balaam finally listens. To appreciate this story, know that talking asses were not at all common in Balaam's day, as they are today. The second point from this story is that now any ass can see, even without the help of an invisible angel, that we are on a perilous energy path.

Like Balaam, we are headed to a very dangerous place, and we must listen to nature to avoid a planetary catastrophe. Nature is an early responder to climate change, and wildlife and fish are especially sensitive to ecological and climatic changes. In a sense, they are speaking to us as they are responding, often poorly, to climate changes. They are important biological indicators of our stewardship performance. In fact, there is a cause and effect relationship between the quality of our stewardship and the fruitfulness of all living resources.

Working as a biologist for the US Fish and Wildlife Service in the late 1940s, Rachel Carson was listening to fish and birds through the data she was reviewing. She was discovering that various groups of wildlife all over the world were shifting their natural ranges and moving quite strikingly and consistently toward the poles. In 1951, in her second book, *The Sea Around Us*, Carson observed, "Now in our own lifetime we are witnessing a startling alteration of climate."[7] Because Carson was listening to nature, she was able to faithfully record fish and bird migratory changes and melting glaciers and rightfully associated these trends with a warming climate. Carson amplified her observations with great detail when she wrote her third book, in 1955. *The Edge of the Sea* again references changing wildlife distribution: "This new distribution is, of course, related to the widespread change of climate that seems to have set in about the beginning of the century and is well recognized—a general warming-up noticed first in the arctic regions, then in subarctic, and now in the temperate areas of northern states."[8] By recording nature's response, Carson pegged the warming pattern to the time frame of the late nineteenth and early twentieth centuries and accurately described its progression from the poles to the equator.

We can learn from fish and wildlife. We must be willing to stop what we are doing long enough to just listen. The evidence is all around us. Decades of complacency and inattention by the media, eight years of stubborn cocksureness by the George W. Bush administration coupled with procrastination and partisan politics of a divided Congress have set the stage for enormous and permanent climatic consequences for wildlife, consequences that are beyond description. Humankind must accept responsibility for the next generation and stop our reckless role in altering the transparency of the earth's atmosphere, a human-caused change that is deregulating the climate system. Because the United States arrives at this moment of action very late, we must do much more much faster than we previously believed in order to establish the right pace to divert a worldwide catastrophe. This is a call for swift action, and bold transformational policies, and visionary leadership.

John A. Brashear, a noted telescope maker, scientist, and humanitarian, once wrote, "The science most worthwhile in this world is that which takes sunlight from behind the clouds and sprinkles it on the shadowed pathways of fellow travelers."[9] My goal is to gather the "sunlight" of evidence distilled from thousands of scientific studies, pull it from behind the clouds of confusion created by fossil fuel interests, and sprinkle the compelling evidence on the shadowed pathways of misdirected travelers who must now join in an all-out effort to end carbon dioxide (CO_2) pollution.[10]

In all matters of significance—material, relational, spiritual, or otherwise—we must seek to discover and embrace truth, regardless of where it may lead. Do not trust a single word I write. Check out every point by seeking truth through the published scientific evidence. Read the scientific literature for yourself. (I provide ample online and published references in the notes and further reading sections for continued digging.) Equip yourself with truth. It is the cornerstone of any ethical system and a sound foundation for action.

But also know that truth can be hard to accept and even harder to live with. The climate debate rages on because many ignore or deny mountains of scientific findings. Global warming also continues to be vehemently challenged because it demands fundamental changes in thinking and behavior. I am reminded of what Winston Churchill once said about truth: "Men occasionally stumble over the truth, but most of them pick themselves up and hurry off as if nothing had happened." Anyone who has not discovered the truth about global warming has not sought the truth in the right places. Willful blindness is a matter of placing political expediency over ethical leadership.

Global warming is not only an intellectual matter, but also a deeply moral and spiritual issue that lets no one off the hook. We must all answer, not just with our best thoughts and words, but with our hearts and actions. We each must see the stark alternatives ahead and choose the right path. By our political and civic actions, we can make a difference in the outcome. It is up to each of us to choose which path we will travel—even if we feel we have to travel alone—in our family, in our workplace, or in our place of worship. After all, in a democracy, stewardship is the duty of each citizen. This is an unabashed call to each and every American to moral duty for the future of life on earth.

If some of the words that I chose appear provocative, I do not apologize. The situation is so grave that I get a lump in my throat when I envision my grandchildren dealing with unchecked global warming. As Proverbs says, "A good man [person] leaves an inheritance for our children's children."[11] For me, that verse now has flesh and blood, feet and hands, and the cute faces of my grandchildren. For the sake of all children, let us work together to solve the climate crisis. They deserve so much better from us.

I come not just with a bunch of facts and figures to aim convincingly at your head. It is with our heads that we think and ponder, while it is from our hearts that we muster courage to act boldly when loved ones are at risk. Let me speak from my heart to yours.

PART I

THE SCIENCE AND THE RAPIDLY APPROACHING REALITY

CHAPTER 1

CLOSER THAN YOU THINK

We are evaporating our coal mines into the air, adding so much carbon dioxide into the air as to change the transparency of the atmosphere. With each passing year, air must be trapping more and more dark (infrared) rays more and more earthlight. Eventually this change might very well heat the planet to heights outside all human experience.

—Svante Arrhenius, 1896

Loud pounding on the apartment door awakened me. Before I could get dressed to answer, the pounding returned. This time it was louder and more aggressive. Throwing my pants on, I raced to discover a firefighter standing in a smoke-filled hallway warning that our building was on fire. He sternly demanded that I leave the building immediately. I did not ask if he was a Republican or Democrat; I did not question his professional judgment or explore for any hidden agenda; I did not seek a contrarian's opinion about the potential of the neighbor's kitchen fire to spread to my unit; nor did I take a wait-and-see attitude about the fire: I followed his advice and got out as fast as I could.

I share this because I see a sharp contrast between how we respond to news of a dangerous structural fire and how we respond to the even greater dangers of global warming. We have been warned about the grave dangers of global warming for a long time. Yet, somehow, the language of scientists has become dangerously obscure, foreign, and unreadable to the average American.

Many talented scientists have done all that they can to get our attention. Great science voices such as James Hansen, Bob Corell, Rosina Bierbaum, Camille Parmesan, Henry Pollack, Tim Flannery, Virginia Burkett, Thomas Lovejoy, Heidi Cullen, Stephen Schneider, Susan Solomon, Katey Walters, George Woodwell, John P. Holdren (the new science advisor to President Obama) and many others referenced in this book have spoken repeatedly, (even very frankly, for scientists) but their urgent messages are not easily reduced to thirty-second soundbites and therefore have not penetrated the nearly impervious American television screen that harbors millions of viewers.

Starting in 1970 with the Study of Critical Environmental Problems conference in Williamstown, Massachusetts, climate scientists have issued multiple warnings with increasing intensity, all saying that we must curb emissions of heat-trapping gases that cause global warming.[1] In 1986 and again in 1987, the Senate Committee on Environment and Public Works invited a number of leading climate scientists from around the world, including top US scientists, to testify at hearings aimed at gaining a better understanding of the state of atmospheric science related to human emissions. In one of those groundbreaking hearings, Wallace S. Broecker, then a geochemist at Columbia University, warned:

The inhabitants of planet Earth are quietly conducting a gigantic environmental experiment. So vast and so sweeping will be the impact of this experiment that were it brought before any responsible council for approval, it would be firmly rejected as having potentially dangerous consequences. Yet, the experiment goes on with no significant interference from any jurisdiction or nation. The experiment in question is the release of carbon dioxide and other so-called greenhouse gases to the atmosphere.[2]

Broecker's warning of grave and immediate danger got my attention. His blunt assessment should have prompted elected leaders to act, and act fast. However, it did not. Here we have an esteemed member of the National Academy of Sciences, a geochemist who has authored eight textbooks in the field and published more than four hundred journal articles, issuing an urgent warning to all inhabitants of planet earth and almost nothing happens.[3]

It's one thing to ignore one author, but the Intergovernmental Panel on Climate Change (IPCC), involving thousands of scientists, has issued four separate reports during the past fifteen years, with the latest report concluding with a "very high confidence that the net effect of human activities since 1750 has been one of warming." Humankind is causing the bulk of global warming with emissions of carbon dioxide (CO_2), methane, and other greenhouse gases.[4] By all reasonable accounts, the core climate science is in, with more than enough published studies pointing to ominous threats in the United States and the world around.[5]

A High-risk Experiment: Massive and Growing CO_2 Emissions

Broecker's assessment at the hearings was right. It is now painfully clear that we are conducting a high-risk, high-consequence planetary experiment outside the range of human experience and competence. Through fossil fuel emissions and through alterations of nature's carbon storage systems, we have elevated atmospheric CO_2 levels by more than 37 percent since the beginning of the Industrial Revolution.

We have all felt radiant heat from an asphalt parking lot baking in the sun. It is that kind of heat that is being blocked from escaping the atmosphere by CO_2 and other global warming pollution. Because CO_2 and other pollutants absorb outgoing long-wave radiation, small amounts of CO_2, nitrogen oxides, or even trace amounts of methane can have a large effect on the planet's heat balance. CO_2 concentrations in the atmosphere have grown from about 281 parts per million (ppm) in the preindustrial age to 387 ppm today, adding a heavy blanket onto the climate system.

Scripps Institute of Oceanography (SIO) scientist Charles Keeling first started tracking this buildup by taking actual measurements at the Mauna Loa Observatory in Hawaii in 1958.[6] In 1970, Charles L. Hosler, then dean of the College of Earth and Mineral Sciences at Penn State University, provided my first exposure to the threat. Back then, when humans were adding about 0.7 ppm of CO_2 into the air each year, Hosler warned, "We are putting astronomical quantities of materials into the atmosphere and there is no question it's affecting the weather. I am afraid the changes are already greater than most people suspect and there may be a threshold beyond which small changes in the weather could bring about a major shift in the world's climate."[7]

CO$_2$ emissions are not stabilizing or going down as anticipated, but are running far higher than the worst-case scenario anticipated at this stage in "Climate Change 2007," the Fourth IPCC Assessment Report. Perhaps the underestimation was caused by a failure to foresee the growth in Asian emissions, which are increasing 5 to 10 percent per year. (Based on the number of coal plants under construction, this will continue for at least another decade.) The underestimation was also caused by the US failure to cut its pollution or even participate in the Kyoto agreement.[8] Black carbon from China's many new and unregulated coal-fired power plants is also amplifying the melt.[9] Soot from China is falling on Arctic and Himalayan ice and snowpack, creating "dirty snow" that increases energy absorption.[10]

The records since 1970 show atmospheric CO$_2$ readings have been climbing year by year.[11] Since the dawn of the Industrial Revolution, the total burden of CO$_2$ in the atmosphere has increased as a direct result of coal, oil, and natural gas usage, deforestation, unsustainable agricultural practices, and other misdirected human activities on the landscape. Collectively, humans are now adding about 2.1 to 2.4 ppm of CO$_2$ pollution into the sky each year. In other words, human activities are netting three times as much additional atmospheric CO$_2$ buildup each year as we were forty years ago.

Reliable estimates of atmospheric CO$_2$ concentrations have been made by drilling and extracting cores from various ice sheets around the world and analyzing the compressed atmospheric bubbles trapped in the annual layers of ice. A compilation of ice bubble data demonstrates that there were about 280 ppm of CO_2 in the earth's atmosphere prior to 1800, and the CO_2 levels varied between 180 and 300 ppm consistently for as far back as ice records extend.[12]

The synthesis report of the IPCC has made it clear that worldwide carbon emissions must be stabilized by 2015 and brought down from current levels in order to make it possible to stabilize CO_2 somewhere between 445 and 490 ppm.[13] To do that and much more, we need to act now. Existing elevated levels of greenhouse gases will continue to trap additional energy, causing future ice melting and ocean warming. Through human alteration of the relationship between incoming solar energy and outgoing radiant energy, the planet continues to warm over time, and the earth is now locked into some rather severe, yet not fully expressed, climate consequences from the thermal blanket that we have already added. In fact, with all of the human-induced changes to the climate system, we should stop calling extreme weather events "acts of God," pretending that we had nothing to do with them.

Fast-moving climate change may soon trigger dire consequences for much of nature and for humankind. World-renowned climate scientist James Hansen of the National Aeronautics and Space Administration (NASA) is known for his straight talk on the matter: "We're toast if we don't get on a very different path." The director of the Goddard Institute for Space Studies (and often called the godfather of global warming science), Hansen warned the Associated Press in 2008 that "this is the last chance."[14] He has repeatedly warned that we must act now before we tip the climate system so far out of balance that we create a fundamentally "different planet."

As Hansen warns, small imbalances can cause big problems. When mechanics build a race car engine, they carefully balance the engine's moving parts to yield maximum horsepower in the form of revolutions per minute (rpm). Depending upon the precision of the balance and other clearance factors, the mechanic rates each engine with an upper rpm limit on the tachometer so the driver knows not to exceed the redline and risk blowing the engine. The earth's tachometer is trying to tell us to take our foot off the gas pedal.[15]

The climate system is out of balance by about 0.5 watt to 1 watt per square meter per year.[16] For every square meter of the earth's surface, excess energy continues to be trapped and eventually either melts ice or accumulates largely as heat in the oceans' waters. In 2007, Hansen warned in testimony before Congress that "if humanity wishes to preserve a planet similar to that on which civilization developed…CO_2 will need to be reduced from its current 385 to at most 350 ppm."[17] If Hansen is correct that 350 ppm CO_2 may be the upper limit, or redline, for the planet, the atmosphere is now over the redline at 387 ppm. If we overshoot that target for very long, we will irreversibly damage life on the earth. Hansen's number makes sense, since it is clear that at 387 ppm, the planet is behaving very badly by shedding ice, killing forests, and releasing methane previously frozen beneath the Siberian Sea and in Arctic tundra into the atmosphere.[18] If anything, Hansen's proposed target may be high, because in the 1940s and 1950s, at much lower CO_2 concentrations, Rachel Carson was already seeing glaciers melting, birds migrating farther north, currents shifting, and fish altering their ranges. Unless we act quickly to stop polluting, to end carbon emissions from oil, coal, and natural gas, CO_2 will continue to accumulate and block additional heat from escaping the atmosphere.

Arctic Melt

The Arctic has been relentlessly melting since the late 1950s. It has lost 40 percent in sea-ice draft, for an overall melt of more than four feet of ice. The data used to make some of these determinations originally came from US Navy submarines, and was gathered using upward-looking sonar to map the extent and thickness of the Arctic ice for purposes of identifying missile launch sites.[19] Now, satellites are able to take ice measurements on a daily basis.

Accelerating Arctic melt may also be caused by changing ocean currents that are sending warm water under the sea ice, altered cloud cover with increased heat-trapping water vapor, or northern transportation of more energy through variable atmospheric transport mechanisms, including more potent cyclones.

Whatever the exact causes of unexpected melt, this vicious cycle is rapidly overheating the region beyond predictions. Soon disappearance of the ice, once seen as impossible, may be an important cause of increased temperature amplification that could alter weather patterns all over the world as its energy-reflecting surface is replaced by a vast expanse of energy-absorbing open Arctic sea.

Rapid Arctic sea-ice melting may be spawning a spiral of related changes that scientists call "positive feedback loops." While scientists understand the phrase *positive feedback loops*, those who use this terminology are not effectively communicating to the public. Calling something positive when it is actually negative baffles people. I much prefer "Arctic amplification" or "dangerous feedbacks" to describe the chain reaction or snowballing that is now occurring.

From the eight-hundred-thousand-year-old ice record, we know that CO_2 and the earth's temperature travel parallel paths. As increased CO_2 warms the planet, a warmer planet emits more CO_2 and methane, which further warm the planet. The spiral is brought on by rather small increases in temperature sufficient to trigger changes in the climate system, which in turn cause more warming.[20]

The increased warming leads to retreating ice, for example, which then leads to additional warming. Melting Arctic ice is an accelerant on other temperature-forcing mechanisms such as permafrost melt, which in turn releases more methane and CO_2, further feeding the vicious cycle.

Scientists can track and project change when it occurs in a straight line or even when it follows a line that curves. Abrupt changes are rarely predictable. The unrepentant melting of the Arctic over the past few decades suddenly accelerated during the summer of 2007. In six days during September 2007, an area the size of Florida melted from the Arctic. The extent and speed of Arctic sea-ice loss reported during the 2007 melt season shocked the world's Arctic and climate scientists, as it set a new modern-day record by shrinking more than 30 percent below previous averages. On December 13, an Associated Press story reported that Mark Serreze, a senior research scientist at the National Snow and Ice Data Center (NSIDC) at the University of Colorado at Boulder, warned that "the Arctic is screaming."[21] Just a day earlier, Wieslaw Maslowski, a research professor at the Naval

Postgraduate School, warned scientists that the Arctic will be ice-free sometime during the summer of 2013.[22] According to his analysis, Maslowski warned that warm water is moving into the Arctic Ocean from the Pacific and Atlantic oceans at much greater rates than the earlier IPCC models predicted.

This rapid melt was not predicted by the Fourth IPCC Assessment Report; they projected summer Arctic ice loss to move more slowly than it has and that the Arctic would be ice-free sometime between 2080 and 2120. The IPCC models were based on reasonable assumptions that the melting of Arctic ice would be more linear, the capacity of natural carbon storage mechanisms such as forests and oceans would be larger and more resilient to saturation, and that nations like the United States would ratify and comply with the Kyoto treaty. Updated predictions of Arctic ice melt now lie outside of the forecasts in the Fourth IPCC Assessment Report by nearly a hundred years. We need to understand the limits of science and be prepared for more climate surprises, because we will have to live with the somewhat unpredictable but undoubtedly dark realities of the feedback loops we've set in motion.

After the dramatic melt in 2007, ice cover remained thinned and weakened in the spring of 2008, with evidence of extensive formations of polynyas in the ice pack. Polynyas are areas of open water surrounded by Arctic sea ice, and they are more abundant in thin and weak ice.[23] Arctic ice has disappeared or become thinner and much more fragile, with a loss of about 70 percent of dense and more durable perennial ice and an increase in the rate of spring and summer melt of vulnerable and thin annual ice.

By the end of the 2008 melt season, NASA and the NSIDC issued the following statement: "The Arctic sea ice cover appears to have reached its minimum extent for the year, the second-lowest extent recorded since the dawn of the satellite era. While slightly above the record-low minimum set in 2007, this season further reinforces the strong negative trend in summertime sea ice extent observed over the past thirty years."[24]

Once nearly the size of the continental United States minus Arizona, floating Arctic sea ice acts as a massive solar energy reflector, bouncing more than 90 percent of the visible light and energy back into space. However, when the floating ice completely disappears in late summer, perhaps sometime within the next five or ten years, the dark ocean waters will absorb about 80 percent of the incoming light and heat energy, which in turn will further warm Arctic waters, altering historic currents and slowing annual Arctic refreezing. As the Arctic loses much of its floating ice in the late summer season, it drastically increases the absorption of heat into the circumpolar region as sunlight-reflecting sea ice vanishes.

Think of the Arctic in its natural condition, as a giant mirror nearly the size of the continental United States keeping the planet cool by reflecting most of the sun's energy back into space. Now imagine replacing that massive mirror with an energy-absorbing dark-surfaced ocean in late summer. It is time for us all to think about the disappearance of that reflector during the summer "minimums" and comprehend its impact on the circumpolar region. Watch for profound and dangerous amplifications that will trigger additional climatic and ecological changes. Scientists monitoring the

Arctic are increasingly worried that the unprecedented melt could mean that climate change has passed at least one ominous tipping point.

One of the most significant impacts of the snowpack and ice loss in the Arctic region is that it also triggers a powerful feedback loop that leads to ever-warmer surface water temperatures, thermal expansion of Arctic waters, and thawing of the region's land-based permafrost. While the Arctic region has warmed, largely a result of retreating sea ice, this warming can penetrate deep inland. It is especially pronounced during the autumn, when sea ice melt is at its nadir and the open ocean waters absorb more than 80 percent of the incoming energy, warming the entire region along the Arctic coasts of Russia, Alaska, and Canada. A recent analysis of observed temperature over the Northern Hemisphere indicates that such an Arctic amplification may already be emerging.[25] According to Bob Corell, chair of the Arctic Climate Impact Assessment, "In Alaska and Canada, winter temperatures have increased by as much as 3–5 degrees Celcius [about 5–9 degrees Fahrenheit] in the past 30 years."[26]

There is a consensus among three hundred scientists, experts, and indigenous elders that the Arctic is being adversely impacted at a rate "more rapidly and persistently than at any time since the beginning of civilization," according to Corell, who like Hansen is not hesitant to talk bluntly about the dangers fraught in our current energy course.[27]

The Arctic region has already warmed to a point where it may be triggering unprecedented changes. Arctic ice coverage plays a crucial role in regulating planetary climate. Some of the world's top climate scientists, including Rajendra K.

Pachauri, the current chair of the IPCC, have warned policymakers that we are on the verge of unleashing several dangerous feedbacks that will snowball into ever more warming at an accelerating pace.[28]

It hardly takes a climate scientist to understand that if all the Arctic ice disappears during the late summer season, weather patterns will likely shift in ways we can scarcely imagine. We need to pay more attention to the importance of jet stream functions in maintaining weather as we have known it. Excess heat caused by Arctic amplification also warms the air over the Arctic and could alter the location, ebb, and flow of the jet stream, with significant implications for major climate systems. In addition, losing the expanse of sea ice covering the Arctic Ocean modifies the exchange of heat and moisture between the ocean and the atmosphere. These exchanges are thought to play a crucial role in controlling the worldwide ocean circulation, with planetary implications for weather and marine wildlife.

METHANE FEEDBACK: FUELING CLIMATE CHANGE

The disappearance of the Arctic ice region creates problems in more than just the air and the water. George M. Woodwell, perhaps the world's leading expert on feedback mechanisms, has warned that "there is a possibility that the warming itself may cause a series of further changes in the earth that will speed the warming."[29] It's not just the warming we have to worry about; we have to think about the many issues that will snowball the effects of the warming and rapidly turn the problem into an unstoppable avalanche. Nowhere is this snowball effect more clear than in the effect the warming has on permafrost. The warmer polar temperatures thaw and decompose vast stores of organic matter locked in nearby shallow permafrost, which in turn release more greenhouse gases into the atmosphere and lead to ever more warming.

Imagine what would happen if your power supply was lost and your freezer full of food thawed out and rotted. As the open Arctic sea absorbs energy, it warms the entire circumpolar region, thawing organic matter stored in the nearby tundra. The tundra's vast carbon reservoirs are decomposing and leaking CO_2 and methane as they thaw more deeply each passing year. There is a lot of organic matter to decay. Permafrost soils, those that remain frozen year-round for at least two years, are now thawing out to record depths across the polar region, unleashing a potentially mammoth new source of global warming pollution. Expected thawing of high-latitude Arctic peat soils is one reason why scientists are worried about tipping points. Widespread high-latitude peatlands respond dramatically to climate change and are significantly increasing the rate of CO_2 and methane escaping into the atmosphere.

Warming is already increasing the decomposition in what scientists call the "active zone" of the permafrost. Scientists are trying to predict what will happen as global warming increasingly thaws permafrost soils at deeper and deeper depths, exposing more and more carbon-containing organic matter to erosion and decomposition.

Deeper permafrost thawing is now a well-documented occurrence. Methane gas leakage is now being detected in the tundra as rapid Arctic warming is breaking down organic matter under wetlands where the absence of oxygen produces methane (anaerobic decomposition). Methane, a greenhouse gas that has twenty-three times the heat-trapping punch of CO_2, is being released from Russia's vast Siberian permafrost, which covers nearly 6 million square miles. Russian scientists who have studied the Siberian region for thirty years have long warned that 70 to 80 billion tons of methane may escape into the atmosphere as the near-surface permafrost thaws in Siberia.[30] In the September 7, 2006, issue of the journal *Nature*, a team of scientists led by Katey Walter of the University of Alaska at Fairbanks published an alarming report.[31] Using new, more accurate measuring devices, they determined that methane is pouring from melting Siberian permafrost at a rate five times what had been projected.

To expand outward from that picture, a paper published in the journal *BioScience* estimated that permafrost blanketing the entire Northern Hemisphere contains 1,672 billion metric tons of carbon, which is more than double the 780 billion tons of CO_2 in the atmosphere today. These findings were a product of a team of nearly two dozen scientists led by Ted Schuur at the University of Florida.[32] In a recent *Yale Environment 360* article titled "Melting Arctic Ocean Raises Threat of 'Methane Time Bomb,'" Pulitzer Prize–winning journalist Susan Q. Stranahan describes the concern: "Arctic soils hold nearly one-third of the world's supply of carbon, remnants of an era when even the northern latitudes were covered with lush foliage and mammoths ranged over grassy steppes. Scientists estimate that the Siberian tundra contains as much buried organic matter as the world's tropical rain forests." Stranahan then emphasizes the extreme urgency and precariousness of this situation, saying, "Ice core studies in Greenland and Antarctica have shown that Earth's climate can change abruptly, more like flipping a switch than slowly turning a dial."[33] With these feedback loops and tipping points added to the global warming picture, we may have less time than anyone—even the most pessimistic—may think.

Arctic sea-ice melt may be causing another secondary tipping point: the release of methane trapped in icelike crystals, called hydrates, beneath the ocean floor. Methane gas hydrates have long been known to exist along the edges of continents in ocean waters about one thousand feet deep. These methane hydrate crystals were formed when buried organisms decomposed in deep, cold water. They stay in place as long as the water temperatures remain cold and water pressures are sufficient to lock the gas in the crystalline hydrate structures. They are also sequestered within the vast Arctic continental shelves in northern Siberia and Alaska and stored deep in permafrost.

These methane hydrates are believed to exist in huge quantities; unconfirmed estimates now range widely between 5.5 and 11 trillion tons in accumulated sediments. Some global estimates of the frozen methane suggest that it is one of the largest stores of hydrocarbons on earth—possibly more than remaining oil and coal deposits combined.[34] Thus a warming of the oceans could trigger a massive release of methane as the crystalline hydrates composed of ice and methane gas relax their hold on the methane.

Methane releases from the Arctic region are exceeding previous predictions, and their potential influence on the climate system creates another significant uncertainty. Climate scientists have long warned that if the vast circumpolar region warmed beyond a certain unknown point, Arctic permafrost and submerged methane-rich hydrates in the oceans could begin to release their stores of methane.

Leading an International Arctic Research Center team, Igor Semiletov has been studying the East Siberian Sea, which is a relatively shallow continental shelf that stretches more than nine hundred miles. A team of scientists on board the Russian research ship *Jacob Smirnitskyi* documented that frozen methane hydrates are now leaking methane. The team took more than one thousand measurements of dissolved methane in the summer of 2008 and found widespread methane bubbles pouring out of chimney formations on the seafloor, indicating that the underwater organic matter was decomposing as submerged permafrost was thawing and that elevated levels of methane were being released from a warming East Siberian Sea.[35] Semiletov said, "The concentrations of the methane were the highest ever measured in the summertime in the Arctic Ocean," and added, "We have found methane bubble clouds above the gas-charged sediment and above the chimneys going through the sediment."[36]

Örjan Gustafsson of Stockholm University described the scale of the methane emissions as "an extensive area of intense methane release."[37] This finding is an urgent warning that human-induced global warming may be pushing nature to give up stores of frozen methane. Until recently, most scientists believed that submerged carbon stores were safely insulated by underwater permafrost, which is on average 11°C warmer than surface permafrost.[38]

Early signs of widespread methane leaking from the East Siberian Sea is not good. This leakage is a matter requiring immediate attention and better scientific understanding about what might be happening elsewhere. Perhaps as a way to collect data from around the world, cargo vessels plying the oceans could be outfitted with auxiliary gas detection monitors that would more accurately record ambient atmospheric methane levels. Linked to satellites, they could create an inexpensive network of early warning methane tracking devices to pick up leakage from other hydrates found along the world's ocean rims. However we can monitor them, we should be paying closer attention to these methane stores.

Looking back through geologic time, another study suggests that methane destabilization was the runaway feedback that rapidly increased warming on earth and ended the last "snowball earth."[39] Martin Kennedy, a professor of geology in the Department of Earth Sciences at the University of California at Riverside noted, "Our findings document an abrupt and catastrophic means of global warming that abruptly led from a very cold, seemingly stable climate state to a very warm also stable climate state with no pause in between."[40] Melting even part of the permafrost and methane hydrates could cause a runaway greenhouse effect.

The Earth Is Losing Its Capacity to Clean the Skies

Boreal forest biome is believed to represent 37 percent of the forest carbon stores on the planet,[41] and roughly 30 percent of boreal forest is located in Canada.[42] Boreal forests survive as a more monocultural forest system in part because their far northern locations allow for bitter cold temperatures to freeze out damaging insects. Cellular frost acts as a powerful insecticide, protecting boreal forest and high-altitude coniferous forests from being ravaged by native bark beetles. However, the warmer winters of recent years have allowed bark beetles and their larvae to survive, start growing earlier in the spring, and cause extensive damage through a longer season. So in recent years, mountain pine beetles have killed more than fifty thousand square miles of forest in western Canada. These pine beetles have already destroyed huge swaths of Canadian boreal forest, largely coniferous forests, and they are on pace to release 270 megatons of CO_2 into the atmosphere by 2020. This happens to be the same amount of greenhouse gas emissions that Canada has committed to reducing by 2012 under the Kyoto Protocol. A team of researchers led by Werner Kurz of the Canadian Forest Service warned that damage from insects "would effectively doom that effort [to control emissions] to failure."[43]

Mountain pine beetles are also destroying millions of acres of coniferous forests in the Rocky Mountain West, because over the past thirty years, western forests in North America have warmed by about 1°F from global warming. The vast quantity of dead wood, combined with higher air temperatures, creates a virtual tinderbox for major forest fires. An SIO study implicates "rising seasonal temperatures and the earlier arrival of spring conditions...with a dramatic increase of large wildfires in the western United States."[44] The institute found a fourfold increase in the number of major forest fires and a sixfold expansion of acres burned in the western United States linked to global warming and drier conditions. Almost seven times more forested federal land burned during the 1987 to 2003 period than during the previous seventeen years.[45]

The warmer temperatures are also triggering widespread hydrological changes, including reduction in snowfall and snowfall accumulations, increased rates of snowmelt, increased evaporation from landscapes, and greater transpiration from trees and plants. Forest soils' moisture levels are a primary indicator of fire danger. Forest soils tend to respire faster as the temperature climbs, giving up more moisture and yielding greater carbon leakage at the same time.[46] Around the world, many forests are experiencing less moisture, earlier snowmelt, warmer average winter temperatures, more insect damage, and increased evapotranspiration rates in summer months.

Warming has triggered large-scale forest fires in recent years, and they have blazed in Corsica, Finland, Sweden, the Czech Republic, Russia, Australia, Africa, and elsewhere. In 2003, Europe experienced one of the hottest summers on record, and a US satellite recorded 157 fires sending plumes of smoke over three thousand miles into the atmosphere, reaching as far away as Kyoto, Japan. About 22 million hectares of mixed forests were scorched by fires that summer. Between 1980 and 2000, the Siberian forests (the largest boreal forest region in the world) experienced winters that were 3.6 to 7.2°F warmer than the pre-1960 norms. Russian forest fires have increased tenfold in the last twenty years, according to Anatoly Sukhinin of the Sukachev Institute of Forest in Russia.[47] In 2004, more than 29 million acres of Siberian taiga burned. (This is the size of my home state of Pennsylvania. I suspect if Pennsylvania burned in a single season, we would have heard about it.)

Expanding fire patterns continue to spread across the Canadian Rockies, in the United States, and in Australia, where a ten-year drought was nicknamed "the big dry." In

2009, a series of brush fires in Australia killed 209 people and injured more than 500. The state of Victoria was hit hard with fires fueled by winds gusting to over sixty mph and temperatures that soared to as high as 120°F. Extreme heat made conditions nearly impossible for firefighters, and entire towns were burned.[48] On February 9, 2009, the Australian Bureau of Meteorology issued "Special Climate Statement 17," which analyzed the exceptional heat wave that affected southeastern Australia during late January and early February and noted that the most extreme conditions were found in parts of Tasmania, Victoria, and areas of New South Wales.[49]

Forests are vital carbon stores necessary for the planet's health. According to a recent study led by the United States Geological Survey (USGS), drought stress, increased forest fires, excess heat, more insects, and increased tree diseases, all brought on by global warming, are causing a pervasive doubling of tree mortality and leading to premature forest death.[50] The study found that "tree death rates have increased across a wide variety of forest types, at all elevations, in trees of all sizes, and in pines, firs, hemlocks and other kinds of trees."

The tree death rate in British Columbia doubled in only seventeen years, whereas tree death in California's old-growth forests doubled in twenty-five years. Native bark beetles alone have killed about 3.5 million acres of lodgepole pines in northwestern Colorado. One of the USGS study researchers, biogeography professor Thomas Veblen of the University of Colorado at Boulder, noted, "The increase in tree mortality rates documented in the study is further compelling evidence of ecosystem responses to recent climate warming." The researchers warned that accelerated forest loss could cause forests to become a net source of CO_2, triggering "an environmental domino effect on the region's wildlife and climate."[51.]

This worldwide pattern of beetle kill, forest fires, and tree death is another dangerous feedback. As vast boreal forest and high-elevation coniferous forests burn, they release massive quantities of CO_2, accelerating climate change even more. As the forests burn, they issue not just vast quantities of CO_2, but more black soot is spewed over distant glaciers, floating ice, and ice-covered landscapes, further accelerating melt.

Tropical rain forests are another important carbon store. These rain forest systems hold enormous amounts of carbon, and they are at increasing risk as well. They continue to shrink in size as a result of timbering and the conversion of forested lands into agricultural land use to feed ever-growing human populations and to offset the loss of agricultural production caused by biofuel production. (As agricultural lands are converted to biofuel production, other lands are converted to agricultural uses to offset food production losses.) Biomass must not be allowed to become the next massive threat to biodiversity and to the remaining forests around the world.

These systems already face enormous threats. Research from the Woods Hole Research Center and other recent studies warn that large tracts of the vast Amazon rain forest ecosystem may be on the brink of irreversible collapse if the drought and other global warming effects on the Amazon continue and if deforestation and fragmentation are not brought into check.[52] This would lead to catastrophic consequences for the world's climate. The Woods Hole study concludes, "As the forest becomes shorter and its canopy more open, compromising its remarkable resistance to fire, it is clear that drought in tandem with fire could swiftly push the tall, dense rainforests of the region towards savanna scrub. The amount of carbon that could be released to the atmosphere by this savannization process is significant—equivalent to several years of worldwide carbon emissions—and could accelerate climate change processes already in place."[53]

A forest report released in April 2009 titled "Adaptation of Forests and People to Climate Change—A Global Assessment" warns that the current carbon-regulating functions of forests are at grave risk of being lost entirely unless carbon emissions are reduced drastically. "With a global warming of 2.5 [degrees] C (4.5 [degrees] F) compared to pre-industrial times, the forest ecosystems would begin to turn into a net source of carbon, [as trees die from drought stress, insect disease, or forest fires and as decomposition of carbon-rich organic matter in forest soils accelerates] adding significantly to emissions from fossil fuels and deforestation." Authored by thirty-five of the world's top forestry scientists, the report provides a sobering depiction of how the world's important forests would react to a continued rise in global temperatures that would trigger severe droughts and heat waves killing off many of the forests in Africa, southern Asia, and South America.[54]

Currently, nearly half of the CO_2 emitted each year is recaptured by nature. Much of it is directly absorbed by the sea or washed out in the rain as weak carbonic acid. The carbonic acid eventually ends up in significant concentrations in the oceans, where it has increased the acidity of the waters.[55] The average ocean-surface pH has decreased by approximately 0.1 units compared to what it was in the mid-1850s.[56] CO_2 released by fossil fuel combustion forms massive amounts of carbonic acid, which creates additional risks for coral, zooplankton, and other creatures that support life on earth. Increasing the acidity of oceans reduces availability of carbonates for shell development and for normal growth of nearly all marine organisms. It has the potential to harm fish, shellfish, and nearly every other form of sea life. According to the IPCC report, "Extinction thresholds will likely be crossed for some organisms in some regions in the coming century."[57]

Though oceans, forests, soils, and other carbon sinks have been absorbing about half of the CO_2 annually emitted, the capacity for nature to remove carbon from the atmosphere is already diminishing. In an article entitled "Carbon Cycle: Sources, Sinks and Seasons," John B. Miller wrote, "We are currently getting a 50 percent discount on the climatic impact of our fossil fuel emissions. Since 1957, and the beginning of the Mauna Loa record of atmospheric CO_2, only about half of the CO_2 emissions from fossil fuel combustion have remained in the atmosphere, with the other half being taken up by the land and ocean. Unfortunately, we have no guarantee that the 50 percent discount will continue."[58]

Scientists have observed the first evidence that the Antarctic Ocean's ability to absorb CO_2 has weakened by about 15 percent per decade since 1981. Paul Fraser, lead researcher of the Changing Atmosphere group at Australia's CSIRO Marine and Atmospheric Research, reported that the international team's four-year study shows that the weakening is due to human activities.[59] Since the oceans are responsible for most of the carbon sequestration, this sharp decline is important, and scary. In yet another global warming feedback, the global carbon drain is threatening to clog.

SLOW-WALKING NEW ENERGY POLICY WHILE THE PLANET RUNS AWAY

A single log sitting on a bed of ashes in a fireplace burns slowly. Add another log, and yet another, and soon the reflective heat from each log causes the others to burn more brightly, casting greater heat. Feedbacks from nature function much like these logs, and are our last warning that the earth is already in the midst of rapid change—a change incomparable in scale and consequence to any other. Nature is experiencing powerful climate consequences caused by the tyranny of billions of misguided and irrevocable energy decisions. Scientists can track and project change when it occurs gradually, but abrupt changes are rarely, if ever, pinpointed by scientists. The rapid Arctic melt of 2007 was an example of such rapid and unpredicted change. The rapid buildup of CO_2 caused by increasing emissions and decreasing sinks is forcing an unprecedented overheating of the bipolar regions beyond all earlier predictions.

Scientists have long debated how the climate would respond to increasing energy-trapping pollutants. Some suggested that the climate would change gradually over time as CO_2 accumulates. Nature, in all of its forms, turns out to be much more sensitive to warming than previously predicted. Increasingly, scientists are warning that there is a possibility that the climate feedbacks outlined in this chapter will cause the climate system to flip quickly to a much warmer state, acting like a single switch or a series of switches flipped in sequence.

Nature gives many examples of abrupt change illustrating this phenomenon. A tree limb bends and bends under a snow load until in an instant it snaps. A mountain snow load in fragile equilibrium gives way under the weight of a single skier traversing the slope and explodes into an avalanche. The web of life is fragile, assembled like a precision watch, with all of its moving parts coming together with small clearances and little tolerances.

The rate of climate change is now unprecedented in recorded human history. Damage to the Arctic ecosystem is outpacing our reparations. Coupled with the loss of terrestrial and ocean sequestration capacity, fast-moving changes from thawing tundra, methane hydrate disruptions, and dying boreal forest and tropical rain forests foreshadow enormous additional CO_2 and methane releases.

Reflecting on the implications of two recent studies, Amanda Staudt, the chief climate scientist for the National Wildlife Federation, warned, "Even if we could turn off the switch on CO_2 emissions immediately, there is no similar switch for turning off warming and other climate changes already put in motion. The climate system has been altered in ways that will be with us for at least 1000 years."[60] According to the work of senior researcher Susan Solomon of the National Oceanic and Atmospheric Administration and her colleagues, long-term CO_2 levels will stabilize at about 40 percent of the peak concentration levels even after emissions have ceased.[61] Surface warming will decline only slightly from what it is when peak concentrations are reached. These findings have major implications for the widely held goal of keeping surface temperatures to no more than 2°F above today's levels and for avoiding the impacts such warming would bring. For example, shifts in precipitation patterns that are already being observed around the globe could become semipermanent. This includes a 10 percent decrease in dry-season precipitation in the southwestern United States, a change that will soon be nearing levels experienced during the Dust Bowl.[62]

When the earth hits certain tipping points, gigantic feedbacks kick in, leading to a runaway climate system triggering unprecedented problems with ecological, food, water, security, and other societal necessities. Something momentous has already been taking place in the polar regions, in circumpolar forests, and on glaciated mountaintops everywhere. Yet most Americans have little inkling of the enormous risks we are taking by ignoring dangerous global warming feedbacks.

Long recorded in numerous science journals accessible to only a few, the fast-emerging impacts of climate change are now becoming clear. Physical evidence is now overwhelming and should be made more accessible for all to see. Rapidly melting glaciers and polar ice, leaking methane from thawing tundra, and burning forests present vivid images needing better interpretation so the public understands how these distant forces will come home and affect our common future.

When a pot on the stove is boiling over, who would propose turning the heat up further? Yet the earth is clearly "boiling over" at 387 ppm, and the accepted thinking among policymakers, based more on political expediency than on scientific considerations, is that we can continue to allow atmospheric CO_2 concentrations to creep up to 450 ppm or even to 550 ppm before we slowly begin to reduce atmospheric concentrations thirty to forty years from now.

Wishful thinking is dangerous. Yet because of difficult and entrenched fossil fuel politics, this is exactly where policymakers are heading with pending legislative plans that allow the CO_2 concentrations in the atmosphere to continue to climb. The difficult choice we face in Washington is to accept and support a bill coursing through Congress that by every measurement may get us started but will not provide sufficient reductions in a timely fashion. Our other option is to oppose its passage and continue to do nothing. Believing that it is easier to turn a wheel on a vehicle that is moving, I have chosen to support a "first-step" bill while urging strengthening amendments. As it stands, the current climate bill will cut emissions by 17 percent within a decade, and I have chosen to support this over continued delay and inaction.

Until more Americans demand bolder actions, we will be stuck with slow reductions while the planet is clearly picking up its pace of change. This is currently true of even the best legislative policies advanced in Washington, DC, as well as the proposed Copenhagen treaty to update and replace the Kyoto Protocol, which expires in 2012.

In a recent speech at the National Press Club titled "Is There Still Time to Avoid 'Dangerous Anthropogenic Interference' with Global Climate?" James Hansen commented on the long history of legislative and administrative inaction: "There is little merit in casting blame for inaction, unless it helps point toward a solution. It seems to me that for far too long, special high-carbon interests have been a roadblock wielding undue influence over elected officials and policymakers."[63] We must stand up and speak up if this roadblock is to be removed.

In ancient times, when cities were the protectorate, watchmen were posted in strategic towers along the outer walls, where they could see great distances and give early warning of an invading army. The book of Isaiah records, "For thus has the Lord said to me: 'Go, set a watchman, let him declare what he sees.'"[64] In this modern world, research scientists in the fields of climate, health, and ecology are our watchmen. They have an important purpose: looking out as far as they can see and reporting any danger that may be on our horizon. Our watchmen have been alert and they have spoken clearly about global warming—repeatedly, for decades.

Our duty is to listen and to get ready for the greatest planetary challenge that has ever confronted humankind. Past societies have badly misjudged the fragility of their environments and naively underestimated the true nature of the catastrophic risks they were creating with misplaced schemes. This pattern is deftly described by Jared Diamond in his book *Collapse: How Societies Choose to Fail or Succeed*.[65] In every societal collapse, there seemed to be little capacity for restraint and a fundamental failure to end destructive practices. A failure to heed warnings today will lead to major tragedies tomorrow. History is bound to repeat itself if we do not change course. We must find the courage and determination to confront the malignancy of climate change.

CHAPTER 2

WHAT HAPPENS IN GREENLAND
WILL NOT STAY IN GREENLAND

Glacial once meant "slow." No longer; glacial ice is now melting and moving at an alarming pace all across the planet. Recent studies suggest that most of the world's nearly one hundred and sixty thousand glaciers have been disappearing, retreating, or degrading during much of the industrial age and adding their meltwater to the oceans of the world.[1] Glaciologists warn that the rate of glacier melting has accelerated dramatically since the mid-1960s.[2] The Himalayas, for example, have massive glaciers that feed into rivers. All the major rivers of Asia flowing from the Himalayas, and the people who depend upon them, are at risk as these glaciers melt:

- Gangotri Glacier flowing into the Ganges River may be gone in twenty years;
- Himalayas and Tibet-Qinghai Plateau glaciers that feed the Indus, Ganges, Mekong, Yangtze, and Yellow rivers are melting at an accelerating rate;
- Tibet-Qinghai Plateau glaciers feeding the Yellow and Yangtze rivers are shrinking at a rate of 7 percent a year.[3]

During heat waves and droughts, surface waters tend to dry up. In times of excess heat, high-elevation glaciers melt faster, augmenting river low-flows and stabilizing water supplies for millions of vulnerable people downstream. In many mountain regions, downstream human populations have become dependent upon excessive meltwater flowing from shrinking and thinning glaciers. China's downstream populations are at risk as the glacially fed rivers are already drying up during droughts.[4]

Wildlife is at risk too. Salmon, trout, steelhead, and other cold-water fish are in jeopardy everywhere glaciers and seasonal snowpacks are shrinking. Their loss means that grizzly bears, bald eagles, and other species that feed on migrating fish will face the same danger. In addition, a National Wildlife Federation (NWF) assessment of the cold-water fish populations in the Northwest concluded that if pollution trends continue, as much as one-fifth of river habitat in the Columbia River basin and other parts of the Pacific Northwest could be too warm for salmon, steelhead, and trout by the 2040s.[5]

Nowhere is the rapid glacial ice melt more dramatic than at the head of the expansive outlet glacier known as Jakobshavn Isbræ near the town of Ilulissat on the west coast of Greenland. Ilulissat is a fishing village with five hundred fishing boats, five thousand people, and nearly as many purebred huskies. Dogsledding on Disko Bay, once the primary means of winter travel, is ending because waters are failing to freeze, even during the winter. According to local officials, Ilulissat has experienced a 9°F rise in average temperature over the past three decades.[6]

Seeing is believing. I talked to many residents of Greenland during my 2007 visit and did not meet a single person who doubted global warming. Day by day, they see it happening, changing the landscapes all around them. Global warming is affecting their way of life, leaving little room for that odd blend of denial, deliberate opacity, and naive underestimation of the influence of CO_2 pollution on planetary functions, reactions we read and hear so much of on blogs and talk radio in the United States.

Greenland's seven hundred and eight thousand square miles of undulating icescapes are unlike any other island landscape. The massive ice sheet covers about 80 percent of the largest island in the world.[7] The ice is about two miles thick, yet it is warming rapidly, particularly in the southern half of the island, where meltwater produces about 4 percent of the annual rise in sea level worldwide.[8] Icebergs are being shed in unprecedented numbers from nearly every glacier around Greenland's coastal margins. Roaring muddy waters rush from the base of crumbling glaciers, feeding torrents of icy-cold muddy water into Greenland's fjords and other waterways, which eventually spill into the ocean. Ice loads in the central region of Greenland are so heavy that they have actually pushed the underlying rock formations below sea level. The point is, there is a lot of ice in Greenland, and it is melting at an increasing pace. The country holds nearly one-twentieth of the world's ice, which, if fully melted, would cause about twenty-one feet of global sea rise.[9]

During my visit to Greenland, at the peak of the 2007 summer season, we watched massive icebergs calving off the high face of the Jakobshavn glacial tongue as the glacier moved about six feet per hour. The calving ice plunged about one hundred feet into the ice-clogged fjord below. Elsewhere, thunderous cracks rattled from massive icebergs as they tumbled, pushed, and shoved each other along a clogged fjord. This one central Greenland glacier is the least stable ice mass in Greenland. It produces far more than its fair share of meltwater. The Jakobshavn drains 8 percent of Greenland's ice sheet, and the ice flow has increased nearly twofold in the last decade.[10]

As the highly reflective ice surface begins to melt in zones where summer warmth turns snow and ice into slush, water drains across the surface until it reaches low-lying depressions and forms supraglacial lakes and ponds, or bodies of water that sit on top of ice fields. The melt zone has dramatically expanded in recent years. In 2004, Bob Corell, chair of the Arctic Climate Impact Assessment, appeared before the Senate Committee on Commerce, Science and Transportation and reported that "over the past two decades, the melt area on the Greenland ice sheet has increased on average by about 0.7 percent a year, or about 16 percent from 1979 to 2002."[11]

Greenland has disproportionately warmed, in part because of supraglacial lake amplifications.[12] Ice surfaces, which reflect 90 percent of the incoming solar energy, have been replaced by supraglacial lakes and black ice, which absorb about 80 percent of the incoming energy. Scientists have long known that supraglacial water bodies act synergistically with climate change and create another feedback. Ongoing studies continue to assess the long-term impact of this amplification to better understand how much surface waters are changing the rate of ice melt and ice movement. Scientists want to chart the net effect more accurately so they can better predict the intensity of the melt, including ice thinning and acceleration of ice flow into the ocean at Greenland's margins.

While in Greenland, I visited the encampment of University of Colorado (CU) at Boulder professor Konrad Steffen, the director of the Cooperative Institute for Research in Environmental Sciences. Steffen has spent an average of seven weeks in the Arctic every summer for twenty-seven years, so he knows the Greenland ice cap. To study ice sheet processes, Steffen's team maintains an extensive remote network of twenty-two monitoring stations known as the Greenland Climate Network. When I visited Steffen, several scientists were conducting research near one of the climate-monitoring stations.[13] These stations transmit data hourly via satellites to CU–Boulder. They also use data from the Defense Meteorological Satellite Program's Special Sensor Microwave Imager/Sounder instruments aboard several military and weather satellites.[14]

The 2007 Greenland melt extent shattered previous records with the largest melt in recorded history.[15] According to Steffen, nearly 19 billion more tons of ice melted during that year than during any other single season since satellite measurements began, in 1979. Steffen also reported that a record amount of surface ice was lost over Greenland during the 2007 season. Large volumes of meltwater are finding ways to escape by forming sheet flows of muddy water and fine sediments that move under the glaciers to natural outlets. A total of 552 billion tons of ice melted off Greenland during 2007.[16] Ten percent more ice melted than in the previous worst year, 2005, according to data gathered from remote monitoring stations at CU–Boulder.[17] That is nearly quadruple the amount of ice that melted just fifteen years ago. Steffen made this comparison: "The amount of ice lost by Greenland over the last year [2007] is the equivalent of two times all the ice in the Alps, or a layer of water more than one-half mile deep covering Washington, D.C."[18]

Meltwater flowing out of temporary ponds and lakes spills onto the adjacent icescapes, cutting vivid braided aqua channels of rushing water that flows along fractures until it finds deep crevasses and spills thousands of feet through moulins, which are internal chutes that carry meltwater down, sometimes a mile or more, to the base of the ice formations, lubricating the surface between the ice and the land below. As a result, sudden widespread movement and breakup of ice is more probable today than it was even a decade ago.

A spectacle is now unfolding in Greenland. Highly lubricated glaciers are moving in several regions of Greenland where horizontal pressures exceed surface friction. Greenland is experiencing a dramatic increase in the number and magnitude of "ice quakes" as large blocks of ice begin to slide into major valleys, draining the Greenland ice sheet. Seismometers worldwide have detected 182 Greenland quakes between January 1993 and October 2005.[19] As various supraglacial lakes dewater and reduce surface loads, the underlying rock below "rebounds" about a foot for every three feet of ice expelled.[20] All of this melting ice and underlying geologic rebound creates the ice quakes.

When the meltwater seeps down through cracks in the ice sheet, it also accelerates the melt by warming the ice from within and, in some areas, allowing the ice to slide more easily over the bedrock below, speeding movement to the sea. Northwestern Greenland, for example, where only one glacial quake occurred between 1993 and 1999, experienced more than two dozen quakes between 2000 and 2005.

As the ice moves, it creates dramatic ice quakes that range from 4.6 to 5.1 on the Richter scale.[21] Göran Ekström, a geophysicist then at Harvard, and his colleagues Victor C. Tsai from Harvard and Meredith Nettles from Columbia examined 136 of the best-documented recent seismic events in Greenland.[22] The researchers found that all of the tremors with low-frequency vibrations came from ice movement originating near outlet glaciers, implicating glacial activity in the seismic disturbances.[23]

Greenland's glaciers are sliding and calving twice as fast as they were five years ago. An eleven-square-mile ice mass (about half the size of Manhattan) broke free from the Petermann Glacier just days before the collapse of seven square miles of the Ward Hunt Ice Shelf off Ellesmere Island, west of Greenland.[24]

New National Aeronautics and Space Administration (NASA) data show that more than 2 trillion tons of land ice in Greenland, Antarctica, and Alaska have melted since 2003.[25] There are various methods to calculate the ice loss in Greenland and to estimate the total tonnage of ice lost annually. The number varies depending upon methodology. According to Waleed Abdalati, head of NASA's Cryospheric Sciences Branch, "While differences in these studies still exist, collectively, they very convincingly paint a picture of the Greenland Ice Sheet as having been close to balance in the 1990s, contributing a small amount to sea level, but becoming significantly out of balance and losing a substantial amount of ice to the sea in the last several years."[26]

Using the current rate of CO_2 growth, some models project long-term melting leading to a complete ice sheet melt over centuries. Such a rise would inundate almost every major coastal city in the world. How fast the melt is occurring continues to be a matter of considerable debate within the scientific community. Melting on Greenland and Antarctica to date is far outpacing earlier predictions by glaciologists.[27]

Several Rhode Island–sized ice shelves have already broken off Antarctica, and there is more than enough meltwater on Greenland to flood all beaches, coastal wetland habitats, and millions of homes and businesses in coastal cities and small coastal communities across the entire planet. According to Kendall Haven of NASA, "Depending on how rapidly such a change occurred, it could be a global-scale catastrophe because nearly one-third of the world's population lives in or near a coastal zone. The global impact of several billion refugees and the negative impacts on coastal economic activity would be staggering."[28] Melting on Greenland alone may be more than double the sea-level projections of the Fourth Intergovernmental Panel on Climate Change report. Bob Corell, the head of the Arctic assessment team, warned that sea levels could rise by 6.5 feet this century.[29]

Sea-level Rise and Vulnerable Wetlands

Coastal systems and estuaries are some of the most productive ecosystems on a global scale and are vital food-producing habitats supporting millions of people.[30] For example, at one time, before it was degraded by pollution and mismanagement, the Chesapeake Bay produced more seafood per acre (largely because of the 154 million pounds of oysters harvested in 1880[31]) than any other place on the planet.[32] The bay was also called "the immense protein factory" by famed Baltimore writer H. L. Mencken in the 1940s, before the great declines in the 1950s.[33]

These systems also provide a number of important ecosystem functions, such as nursery areas for shell- and finfish populations, bird and waterfowl habitats, storm surge protection, and nature conservation. Coral reef, wetland, sea grass, and shellfish bed loss can have a significant human cost, even if those directly affected do not always perceive this loss until it's too late. Imagine going to the beach for summer vacation and finding the beaches gone and no seafood restaurants. It sounds far-fetched, but may not be far from the truth if attitudes and practices do not change. Some suggest that a fundamental change in environmental attitudes about wetlands may have the most important implications for the future of coastal wetlands, perhaps even more than fear of the magnitude of various twenty-first-century sea-level rise scenarios.[34] We must help the public and policymakers better understand the many unheralded ecosystem services that coastal wetlands provide to ocean fisheries, to coastal protection, and to the protection of millions of coastal residents so that they will see the value in restoration investments.

Sadly, with massive federal flood insurance subsidies and nearly nonexistent enforcement of the Clean Water Act, protection for all types of wetlands has declined across the United States. According to the Environmental Protection Agency, the Lower 48 have lost more than half of their original wetland acres.[35] Coastal wetlands as one element of that estimate continue to be prime development sites and are declining rapidly, primarily through direct human encroachments. Hence, significant continued losses are possible even without climate change, but these fragile and disappearing systems will be severely damaged by human-induced sea-level rise.[36]

Continued rise in sea levels will increase the depth of coastal waters, forcing salinity intrusion inland and upstream, affecting freshwater and brackish-water wetlands as well as many surface and coastal groundwater supplies. Critically important ecological components of coastal habitats are at great risk for inundation, including salt marshes, mangrove swamps, unvegetated salt flats, mudflats and sandbars, intertidal shorelines, and all estuarine, coastal freshwater, and brackish-water wetlands.

Depending somewhat upon changes that may occur to coastal rainfall amounts and uncertain and more variable future river flows, sea-level rise will undoubtedly alter most brackish-water estuaries, causing them to become more saline. A rise in sea level would increase the size and salinity zones of estuaries, bays, and coves and may increase the salinity of coastal aquifers up the Hudson, Delaware, and Potomac rivers and along other river systems affected by tidal flows. For example, we should expect a more saline and enlarged Sacramento–San Joaquin Delta.[37] Cities such as Philadelphia, Miami, and New Orleans—and nearly every other coastal community—may need to step up efforts to combat salinity intrusion.

Perhaps the most alarming statistic about this situation is that Louisiana's coastal wetlands are disappearing into open water at a rate of up to fifty square miles per year.[38] The United States' largest and perhaps most valuable wetland community is losing its marshes and swamps to the Gulf of Mexico, largely as a result of poorly designed shipping lanes in the Mississippi River, ill-placed shipping canals, the dredging of canals for the withdrawal of oil and gas, flawed flood-control levees, and the subsidence of lands from sea-level rise and oil and gas extraction. This will accelerate if sea-level trends continue.

Louisiana's coast has long supported one of the nation's unique bilingual cultures, 25 percent of the nation's remaining fishing industry, and North America's largest fur-producing industry.[39] Its loss will force more than 2 million people who live in coastal parishes, which generally lie within two feet of sea level, to flee their homes and communities. Without fast action to stop polluting and start coastal restoration, as sea levels rise, unique coastal ecosystems will be mostly lost in this centuy. Yet, knowing the risks ahead, not a single Louisiana lawmaker from either party supports climate legislation that would curb CO_2 pollution and protect coastal Louisiana. Big Oil, with many coastal refineries, dominates politics there. When Big Oil has spoken, Louisiana's lawmakers on both sides of the aisle have listened, often to the detriment of their communities.

Protective wetlands around New Orleans have experienced catastrophic saltwater intrusion from sea-level rise and from a flawed Army Corps of Engineers canal construction project that killed the famous cypress swamps that once protected New Orleans. Thus, a wide array of Lower Ninth Ward community groups understand perhaps better than most the importance of restoring natural resilience. They are partnering with local government agencies to rebuild natural storm buffers. Treated wastewater flushed into the wetlands will help reduce salinity, increase nutrients, and restore the hydrologic conditions that once protected New Orleans before the unnecessary ship canal was dredged. The group plans to restore thirty-one thousand acres of cypress forest in the Bayou Bienvenue–Central Wetlands Unit, which will one day provide much needed protection from storm surges. By piping treated sewage discharges, stormwater, and river sediments onto the delta and planting cypress seedlings, the group hopes to accelerate the natural process.

This habitat restoration project exemplifies how restoring nature protects human communities. Funding from pending climate legislation must provide rational solutions to important ecological threats. By funding coastal restoration projects like the ones in the Lower Ninth Ward, we can safeguard our country's natural resources while protecting vulnerable communities.

Another example of where habitat restoration is essential is in the Chesapeake Bay, where low-lying, vulnerable Eastern Shore communities and their associated wetlands will be especially threatened by rising tides.[40] A recent assessment of sea-level rise, issued by the NWF, concluded, "Coastal habitats in the Chesapeake Bay region will be dramatically altered if sea levels rise globally about two feet by the end of the century, which is at the low end of what is predicted if global warming pollution remains unaddressed." More than 167,000 acres of undeveloped dry land and about 161,000 acres of brackish marsh would be lost, replaced in part by over 266,000 acres of newly open water and 50,000 acres of salt marsh. Ocean and estuarine beaches also will fare poorly, declining by 58 percent and 69 percent, respectively, by 2100. In addition, more than half of the region's important tidal swamp is at risk. Coupled with increasing human population, pollution, and development pressures, losses of land to sea-level rise will put Chesapeake Bay habitats at greater risk unless proactive measures to protect vulnerable lands are put in place."[41]

The need for immediate and bold action to protect the coastline is much greater than previously thought. Yet the possibility that sea level may eventually rise three feet by midcentury is not a reason to lose hope or give up efforts to protect and restore coastal environments such as Louisiana's wetlands. Instead, it is reason to demand implementation of new sediment distribution measures along the lower Mississippi to restore the delta's former ability to distribute muddy water and allow sedimentation and other processes to keep pace with subsidence and sea-level rise. Long-term plans must obviously consider the latest projections in the rise of sea level that are expected to occur in the next fifty to one hundred years and look at the feasibility of reinflating spent oil and gas formations with compressed CO_2 where the formations can be reliably secured. Only by restoring natural accretion using Mississippi River sediments and perhaps by reinflating depleted oil and gas fields with CO_2 can we avoid some of the losses caused by rising sea levels and intensified coastal storm impacts.

Most importantly, coastal residents and those who have an affinity for healthy, natural coastal communities must look beyond the opacity created by oil and coal company advertisements and comprehend what is now happening in Greenland,

Antarctica, and on thousands of glaciers. Accelerating melt coupled with warming and expanding ocean waters will redefine coastlines, coastal communities, and natural coastal systems. Robert Repetto, a retired economics professor from the Yale School of Forestry and Environmental Studies, wrote a paper titled "The Climate Crisis and the Adaptation Myth." In it, Repetto warns that "reactive adaptation would be likely to lag persistently behind the emerging risks. The more rapid the rise in atmospheric concentrations, the faster the rate of climate change and the less effective reactive adaptation is likely to be."[42] Repetto is right; we must proactively protect communities by reclaiming coastal wetlands and by planting mangroves or cypress trees as buffers against storm surges. Coastal areas should be restored to wetlands where practical.

Unless world leaders commit to aggressively implementing pollution controls, agricultural and forest sequestration measures to restrain growing atmospheric CO_2 concentrations, and legislate the enforced use of carbon-negative fuels, coastal regions, with their high-hazard human developments, will be forced back from the coastal edge as sea levels rise and fierce storms increase. Every major coastal city and small town on tidal waters, even those that are far from the ocean such as Washington, DC, Philadelphia, and Baltimore, must beware. What is happening in Greenland will not stay in Greenland.

WHAT YOU CAN DO: PROTECT AN ECOSYSTEM NEAR YOU

We all live in or near an ecosystem that is under siege from a range of conventional threats including land fragmentation, pollution, and myriad other habitat stresses. These important places face additional and perhaps catastrophic threats from mounting climate stresses.

As we confront a warming world, it is important to understand all existing threats to ecosystems in order to remove as many risks as possible. You can help build greater resilience into an ecosystem near you. It may not be possible to protect every species from every threat, but, by working together with others, we can:

1. Plant trees and install cattle fences to restore buffers along streams and rivers
2. Remove human encroachments and restore degraded wetlands
3. Link fragmented habitats with wildlife corridors to create wildlife escape routes
4. Facilitate northward migrations of threatened plants and animals by removing barriers and helping nature adapt to a warmer world
5. Cushion wildlife impacts from a warming landscape by ensuring sufficient cover from the heat and minimizing water withdrawals from rivers, lakes, and streams

You can also do your part by:

1. Making sure your flood insurance is up to date if you live near the coast or along tidal rivers, or, better yet, moving away from high-risk coastal locations
2. Joining national or local efforts to protect remaining coastal habitats; restore mangrove swamps, cypress swamps, wetlands, and other coastal buffer systems; and support efforts to educate others about the importance of these buffer ecosystems
3. Urging Congress to
   a. Require that flood protection maps be updated and made more accurate by using the latest climate modeling rather than relying on outdated historic records
   b. End all federal subsidies, including flood insurance, that encourage people to make sub-prime investments in dangerous places
   c. Empower and fund the US Army Corps of Engineers to restore coastal habitats and thereby reduce dangerous storm surges, rather than building canals and other projects that increase risks

PART II

THE VICTIMS, THE PERPETRATORS, AND THE ENABLERS

Chapter 3

STRUGGLING ECOSYSTEMS
ARE FACING GLOBAL WARMING

Preferring the clear, cool waters of Lake Erie's deeper central and eastern basins, the famed blue pike was a large fighting fish found in extravagant abundance.[1] This fighting spirit, along with being a culinary favorite, made the blue pike an important target for commercial and sport fishing in Lake Erie, Lake Ontario, and the upper Niagara River. Commercial and recreational fishermen harvested over a billion pounds of blue pike between 1885 and 1962.[2]

However, the extinction of the blue pike was not caused only by overfishing. Seldom do such ecological tragedies spring from a single event. If fact, many compounding factors conspired to trigger this extinction, including habitat degradation, invasive species, and persistent, hypoxic (low oxygen) conditions in the western and central basins of Lake Erie caused by excess nutrient loadings and pollution. The unintentional introduction of nonnative species, such as sea lamprey through the Welland Canal, and the intentional introduction of nonnative sport fish may have also contributed.[3] Sadly, all of these events combined to force the extinction of Lake Erie's once-famed blue pike.

As the unregulated fishing industry was peaking in the mid-1960s, sewage and other pollution also peaked. Increasing volumes of raw and undertreated sewage spewed from every city around Lake Erie and from all the other Great Lakes cities. At the time, biologically available phosphorus, the underlying cleaning agent in most detergents, was determined to be the limiting nutrient that regulates the total amount and density of algae that a lake can produce.[4] With the sewage providing phosphorus in staggering abundance, the production rate of phytoplankton (mainly free-floating algae) increased 2,400 percent from 100 per milliliter in 1927 to 2,500 per milliliter in 1964. With 13 million residents flushing about 174,000 pounds of phosphorous into the lake daily, algae blooms peaked and then sucked oxygen from the water as the dead algae decomposed, turning the lake from a clear blue to a pea green and triggering repeated fish kills. Too much phosphorus meant too much algae, and that led to too little oxygen.

Hypoxia, or lack of dissolved oxygen, had been prevalent in the central basin of Lake Erie throughout the middle of the twentieth century, but that condition spread, and low-oxygen levels eventually reached the eastern basin as well. This expansion stressed and eventually devastated the blue pike's critical spawning habitat. Because of their deep-water preferences, blue pike were especially susceptible to low-oxygen "dead zones" deep in the lake.

Because of these conditions, pollution-caused eutrophication became the knockout blow on top of a series of other destructive hits to Lake Erie's once extravagantly abundant fishery and contributed to the loss of its crown jewel, the blue pike.[5] The last recorded successful spawn of blue pike was in 1954, and by 1958 the fishery had collapsed. By 1965, eleven short years after the last spawn, the last confirmed specimen of blue pike was caught from Lake Erie.[6] The US Fish and Wildlife Service officially declared the blue pike extinct in 1976, and no other fish has moved into the blue pike's deep-water ecological niche since then.[7]

In addition to raw sewage, Lake Erie was being overwhelmed by toxic industrial wastes from steel mills, tire manufacturers, and many other outlets. Untreated industrial discharges were prevalent during the region's industrial heyday.[8] The Cuyahoga River is one of Lake Erie's tributaries and flows south from above Akron through the industrial districts of Akron and Cleveland and then north into Lake Erie. This river was so polluted with industrial wastes that it had a bad habit of catching fire. It burned on ten different occasions during the region's booming manufacturing years. The last big river fire was on June 22, 1969, when oil-laden debris floating on the Cuyahoga erupted into flames.[9] The river rapidly became the poster child for the proposed clean water bill pending in Congress and drew national attention when sparks from a passing train ignited the oily slick and debris on the river and roaring flames damaged bridges above. On August 1, 1969, *Time* magazine graphically described the polluted condition of the Cuyahoga River:

> Some river! Chocolate-brown, oily, bubbling with subsurface gases, it oozes rather than flows. "Anyone who falls into the Cuyahoga does not drown," Cleveland's

citizens joke grimly. "He decays." The Federal Water Pollution Control Administration dryly notes: "The lower Cuyahoga has no visible life, not even low forms such as leeches and sludge worms that usually thrive on wastes." It is also—literally—a fire hazard.

For many years, Cleveland's river fire became the butt of Johnny Carson's late-night television jokes as the city became known as one of the most polluted and degraded in the United States—all because its leaders yielded to the influences of polluters and failed to take care of the city's river, waterfront, or air quality.

In response to widespread public protest and extensive media coverage on both sides of the border, the United States and Canada signed the Great Lakes Water Quality Agreement in 1972. The agreement emphasized the need to reduce phosphorous loadings into Lake Erie and Lake Ontario. At about the same time, many grassroots clean water campaigns finally paid off when Congress, after more than twenty years of halfhearted measures and empty promises, finally passed a powerful clean water act. President Nixon vetoed it because he thought it was too bold and because it authorized $18 billion in federal assistance to clean up US sewage treatment plants, including those feeding into Lake Erie. With a strong reaction and push back from concerned Americans, Congress finally mustered enough votes to override the president's veto and passed the Federal Water Pollution Control Act Amendments of 1972. The so-called Clean Water Act became law without Nixon's signature. He responded by "impounding" the funds for the sewage treatment.

At the time, I was a young staffer for the Pennsylvania legislature that fostered the formation of the Interstate Legislative Committee for Lake Erie. In March 1973, the multistate committee gathered in Washington, DC, to appeal to Gerald Ford, the Republican minority leader from Michigan, to see if he could help us convince the president that the sewage funding was desperately needed to restore Lake Erie. Ford, an avid angler and a pragmatic moderate Republican, was sympathetic to our request but doubted that he could move the president on the issue. It was apparent that Nixon had his hackles up over the veto override.

Things took a couple of surprising turns in our favor when on October 10, 1973, Spiro Agnew, to escape time in jail for taking bribes, pleaded no contest to a charge of income tax fraud and resigned the vice presidency. Gerald Ford was appointed vice president, and then on August 9, 1974, he became president as a result of Watergate. President Ford soon ended the long, drawn-out battle for clean-water funding. With substantial federal assistance, every major city around Lake Erie constructed sewage facilities, providing the long-awaited pollution abatement by cutting every significant phosphorous point source discharge into Lake Erie to a concentration of no more than one milligram per liter of water. The cleanup was too late for the blue pike, but the treatment strategy substantially reduced lake algae by controlling the limiting nutrient phosphorus.

The protracted and tedious legislative process to pass a strong clean water law with federal funding assistance was riddled with political delays that cost Lake Erie dearly. Since point source discharges were eventually better controlled, the pollution abatement kept much of the original biodiversity intact, including native cold-water species (lake herring and lake white fish), and other species recovered as water quality improved. While no fish can replace the blue pike, other nonnative fish and shellfish have moved into Lake Erie, perhaps in part since pollution severely stressed natives and physically altered the lake's habitat.

INVASIVE SPECIES TAKING OVER DAMAGED ECOSYSTEMS

Years ago, I inadvertently brought home a copperhead that was hibernating inside a hollow piece of firewood. Fortunately, I captured the awakened and unhappy hitchhiker before it could bite one of my daughters, who had been sitting on the pile of firewood. In much the same way, our international trade introduces unwanted and destructive hitchhikers.

Zebra mussels, for example, are now moving freely across the globe, leaving an unprecedented trail of ecological destruction and economic loss in their wake. Since the construction of the navigational canal, most invasive species have come into Lake Erie in the ballast water of ships as they bypassed the natural barrier of Niagara Falls. Zebra mussels are aggressive mollusks that colonize on hard subsurfaces and profoundly damage lakes and rivers by altering nutrient cycles and by displacing native fish and shellfish. Zebra mussels are believed to have caused a 65 percent drop in lake trout populations in Lake Erie alone. Oceangoing ships now navigating the lakes have discharged exotic zebra mussels that perhaps more than any other single invasive species have transformed the character of Lake Erie as they exploded in number. The mussels cleared the lake of much of its algae, and they have also crowded out bottom-dwelling native species, clogged water and sewer pipes, covered underwater features, and coated hard surfaces and other submerged structures.

It was once hoped that toxins deposited during the unregulated industrial days would eventually be permanently buried in the deep lake sediments. As bottom-dwelling filter feeders, the zebra mussels reactivate and increase the concentration of most waterborne contaminates that have settled to lake-bottom sediments within each successive link in the food chain. The zebra mussels also pick up and amplify atmospheric mercury that is spewed at dangerous levels from coal-fired power plants and deposited in the lake.

The explosive growth of zebra mussels has also led to the explosive growth in another invasive species, round gobies. Also imported into the Great Lakes as a hardy hitchhiker in unregulated ballast waters, ugly and pugnacious gobies entered western Lake Erie in 1994, probably originating from either the Black or Caspian sea.[10] Since their arrival, these invasive bottom-dwelling fish have dominated all three basins of the lake. Gobies are voracious feeders, eating zebra mussels, native snails, aquatic insects, and the young of other deepwater bottom-dwellers such as sculpins, darters, and logperch. A single goby can eat as many as seventy-eight zebra mussels per day and by doing so amplifies the full spectrum of elevated toxins accumulating in the zebra mussels.[11] Round gobies have caused substantial damage to the native fishery by consuming much of the benthic prey and by uptaking and further concentrating and biomagnifying toxins found in zebra mussels. By 2001, an estimated

10 billion round gobies dominated western Lake Erie, eating a staggering twenty-five thousand tons of biomass.[12] By biomagnifying contaminants, zebra mussels and gobies are changing the levels of phosphorus and dangerously altering the concentrations of toxins such as mercury.[13]

In addition to mercury, coal emissions still include acid-forming sulfur oxides (SO_x) and nitrogen oxides (NO_x), which create acid rain. These health-threatening toxic metals further concentrate through filter-feeding zebra mussels, which act much like underwater vacuum sweepers. The toxins are further amplified by mussel-eating gobies and biomagnified again through the sport fish that eat the ubiquitous gobies.[14] By feeding on gobies, Lake Erie's walleye, bass, and other recreational fish have become highly contaminated with mercury and other toxins that originated largely from coal-burning power plants and were washed out of the sky by precipitation. Dangerous, persistent toxins, heavy metals, and other bioaccumulating pollutants move up the food chain in greater and greater concentrations at each step and are eventually ingested by humans who consume the sport fish.

Despite the obvious danger to humans, most of the coal industry and many coal-burning utilities have fought congressional and administrative efforts to scrub toxic pollutants from their flue gases and to capture, sequester, and safely store carbon emissions. Until better laws and rules are adopted, SO_x, NO_x, mercury, and other toxic pollutants from coal-burning power plants will continue to accumulate in the lakes and feeder streams as they have for decades.[15] And as they continue to accumulate, the sport fish will become more and more dangerous for human consumption.

Round gobies and zebra mussels are just a few of the more than 132 known nonnative and invasive species that inhabit the Lake Erie watershed. Like those two species, most arrived from unregulated ballast waters and are having an effect upon the Great Lakes ecosystem. There are now twenty species of nonnative algae, three new disease pathogens, twelve nonnative mollusks, eight nonnative submerged plant species, thirty-nine new marsh plant species, five nonnative trees and shrubs, nine new species of worms, nine nonnative crustaceans, four other invertebrate species, and twenty-three imported fish species.[16] These numbers are conservative estimates, as new species continue to be found.[17]

A DEGRADED LAKE ERIE FACING A WARMING WORLD

In 1971 when Barry Commoner, a renowned cellular biologist and pioneering environmental advocate, warned that Lake Erie was dying, he was sharply criticized for overstating the matter. Facing charges that he was exaggerating the pollution problem, Commoner stood by his assessment, saying, "I believe that practically speaking Lake Erie will never be returned to anything approximating the condition it was in, say, twenty-five to fifty years ago."[18] While Lake Erie has seen significant recovery in terms of water quality, it turns out that Commoner was right and his critics were dead wrong. Lake Erie is now biologically a vastly different lake than it was only half a century ago.[19]

Lake Erie, like so many other damaged freshwater ecosystems around the world, is facing the enormous threat of global warming with its natural resources compromised by pollution and overfishing and with little habitat resiliency in reserve. These ecosystems are extraordinarily important habitats for freshwater species. Despite their impairments, they still hold about 25 percent of the world's vertebrate species yet cover less than 1 percent of the earth. US freshwaters hold 60 percent of the known crayfish species, 30 percent of the freshwater mussel species, 40 percent of the stonefly species, and 30 percent of the known mayfly species.[20]

Lake Erie will continue to face changes as the climate of the Great Lakes region shifts. Winters are getting shorter. Annual average temperatures are growing warmer. Extreme heat events occur more frequently. The duration and average extent of lake ice cover is decreasing as air and water temperatures rise. Heavy precipitation events, both rain and snow, are becoming more common, and intense runoff washes increasing quantities of sediment and surface pollutants into the lake.[21]

From 1898 to 2002, Lake Erie's winter ice has been declining in terms of both average ice coverage and duration.[22] As ice cover declines, lake-effect snow patterns have changed throughout the Great Lakes region, actually increasing snowfalls in some communities. Lake Erie's water temperature has already increased by an average of 1°F since 1988, and the Lake Erie Management Plan predicts that water levels could fall about thirty-four inches as the region warms.[23] The plan also predicts that Erie's surface area will shrink by up to 15 percent as continued warming triggers steep drops in water levels over the next sixty-four years.[24] These are major changes, and they will amplify the stress on a lake that has been mistreated for decades.

On Lake Erie today, the water is heavily filtered by zebra mussels and looks beautiful—clear and clean to the casual observer. However, the combination of existing ecological stressors and global warming will be a very dangerous duo. Various warnings presented in the most recent reports of the Intergovernmental Panel on Climate Change stimulate poignant memories as scientists warn of a staggering rate of extinction in the years ahead. Images of a pea green Lake Erie are stored in my mind's eye along with the painful memory of an extinct fish. These images come flooding back as I see new warnings of algae blooms and a growing hypoxic zone in a warming, shallow Lake Erie. If the future is not clear everywhere, it is here, on the shores of a lake visited by death: we must be proactive to protect and restore fragile ecosystems facing global warming. Otherwise, there may be no turning back.

Most people living near Lake Erie today have forgotten or never knew about the blue pike. But old-time anglers remain a hopeful lot. Rumors persist on angler websites, blogs, and among older anglers who frequent the tackle shops, that someone somewhere caught a blue pike. (I guess it is true that all anglers tend to be optimists.) Ever wishing for an eventual discovery and reintroduction of the blue pike, they search longingly for an overlooked remnant population—perhaps in some remote Canadian lake. Many, it seems, loved the blue pike as a tasty fish, but like so many other species, it was not cherished as a fragile living resource that could be lost in an instant. Sadly, the once magnificent blue pike is extinct. Barring a miracle, extinction is forever.

CHAPTER 4

ON THIN ICE

The air temperature was well below zero. My heart felt as though it stopped for a few seconds as I plunged into the frigid, icy waters. There we were, two teenage boys, thrashing around in a hole cut through the thick ice, each unwilling to be the first out. I do not remember who exited first, but I remember this: I have never been as cold as I was when Wes Braunbeck and I joined the Polar Bear Club—that rather exclusive, old-world club of fools, each crazy enough to swim in icy waters on New Year's Day.

With vivid memories of those icy waters and a deeper respect for the real polar bears, I write about these majestic mammals that, until recent years, were well adapted to one of the most hostile, mysterious environments on the planet. Having thrived in the Arctic for more than one hundred thousand years, polar bears are highly specialized for their unique environment, which is rapidly melting away.[1] Polar bears can swim up to about six miles per hour in frigid Arctic waters.[2] Because these adept swimmers have about four inches of fat over their entire body, they can swim up to sixty miles and survive in water colder than that in which I nearly froze in minutes.[3]

The word *awesome* is overused and often misapplied in contemporary vernacular. However, in describing charismatic polar bears, awesome is nearly an understatement. Fierce carnivores, a polar bear will stalk and kill a one-hundred-and-fifty-pound ringed seal with a single pounce. These creatures will feed on young walruses and other animals when given a chance, but they survive almost entirely by hunting ringed and bearded seals. As seals emerge from *atluks* (air holes) in the floating Arctic ice, a quick swipe of one of the bear's powerful forelegs is usually lethal.

Superbly adapted to the frigid Arctic ice and snow, polar bears are the principal predator at the top of the Arctic marine food chain. To maintain viable breeding numbers, polar bears must inhabit and hunt in their true home, amid the floating Arctic ice. But as the entire Arctic ecosystem goes, so goes the polar bear. Since polar bears hunt from floating ice, the alarming loss of sea ice coverage has profound implications for this sentinel wildlife species and all other species that share this stark ice habitat. As Arctic sea ice breaks up and floes drift south into the North Atlantic Ocean earlier and earlier each year, polar bears must swim farther and farther to find remaining ice or move deeper into the Arctic coastlands to forage where they are less adept hunters. Although some bears may survive there, local hunting guides in northern Canada have reported that the bears appear food-deprived and more aggressive.[4]

Safe habitat will soon be completely out of their reach in much of the Arctic. As summer ice melts, polar bears are forced to swim greater and greater distances to safety, burning their needed fat reserves. Nine polar bears made national news when they were spotted swimming north in the Chukchi Sea off Alaska's northwest coast during the summer of 2008. They were swimming where ice should have been.[5] The bears ranged from fifteen to sixty-five miles offshore and were headed north to the nearest ice, which, unknown to them, was four hundred miles away. Even if they eventually made it to safety, which is highly doubtful, they were at great risk of having their fat reserves completely depleted so that they would be unable to reproduce successfully. While their fate is unknown at this time, there was little likelihood of survival.

As these magnificent animals are stranded in hostile Arctic waters, some will be forced into more southern, land-based habitats, where their highly specialized hunting technique is a hindrance to long-term survival. Many stranded bears will die prematurely from the long-term effects of depletion of fat reserves, fatigue, and lack of food.[6] Andrew E. Derocher, an internationally renowned polar bear expert formerly from the Norwegian Polar Institute in Tromso (he now serves as the leading polar bear researcher at the University of Alberta), cautions, "As the sea ice cracks and drifts more on wind and current, the bears are effectively on a treadmill that humans are steadily increasing in speed. The more energy that is used for locomotion, the less energy there is for growth and reproduction."[7]

As they move south, polar bears compete with grizzly bears or simply fail to get sufficient food for successful reproduction. Bears with lowered body mass have difficulties sustaining cubs. According to the US Fish and Wildlife Service, "The western Hudson Bay population of polar bears in Canada has suffered a 22 percent decline." About nineteen polar bear subpopulations are described in the circumpolar Arctic.[8] Assessing the impact of habitat loss on polar bear populations, a recent study by the USGS Alaska Science Center discovered a "very dramatic" change in cub survival and estimated that as a result of shrinking ice habitat, as few as 43 percent of the polar bear cubs in Alaska's Beaufort Sea are surviving their first year.[9] Cub survival was down from about a 65 percent survival rate, measured in the late 1980s and early 1990s.[10]

A Reluctant Decision-maker and Wrong-headed Rulemaking

On February 16, 2005, the Center for Biological Diversity (CBD) filed a petition to list the polar bear as a threatened species under the Endangered Species Act. Because the law requires a preliminary finding on the listing petition within three months and no action had been taken after ten months, the CBD joined the Natural Resources Defense Council and Greenpeace in seeking to force action on the petition.[11]

The government eventually made a preliminary finding that listing the polar bear warranted a full-scale review, but then it missed the subsequent deadline for making a formal proposal to list (or not list) the species and invite public comment. Additional litigation ensued. Meanwhile, Congress held hearings before the Senate Environment and Public Works Committee, including one in April 2008 at which the National Wildlife Federation's (NWF) senior scientist, Doug Inkley, testified in support of listing the polar bear as a threatened species. Finally, after numerous lawsuits, congressional hearings, and some six hundred thousand public comments, the vast majority of which supported the listing, on May 14, 2008,

Secretary Dirk Kempthorne begrudgingly declared the polar bear a threatened species under the Endangered Species Act. While the Bush administration took a series of actions to ensure that oil and gas exploration (made more accessible by the melting ice pack) continues unfettered in the polar bear's habitat, the polar bear became the first mammal ever listed under the Endangered Species Act for climate-related reasons.[12]

As weak as the polar bear listing was, it was still opposed by Alaska's governor Sarah Palin, who challenged the Bush administration's decision to list polar bears as a threatened species under the Endangered Species Act. Governor Palin wrote an opinion piece in *The New York Times* on January 5, 2008, that read in part, "There is insufficient evidence that polar bears are in danger of becoming extinct within the foreseeable future—the trigger for protection under the Endangered Species Act." Palin's position was not to defend polar bear hunting, as some have suggested, but to maintain oil and gas development in onetime prime polar bear habitat off Alaska's northernmost coasts. In the same opinion piece, the governor acknowledged, "We have a ban on most hunting—only Alaska Native subsistence families can hunt polar bears—and measures to protect denning areas and prevent harassment of the bears."[13]

On August 4, 2008, just weeks before she became John McCain's unequally yoked running mate, Governor Palin announced that Alaska had filed a lawsuit in the US District Court for the District of Columbia seeking to overturn the decision to list the polar bear as threatened under the Endangered Species Act. The governor issued a statement at the time of the filing stating that "the unwarranted listing of the polar bear as a threatened species will have a significant adverse impact on Alaska by deterring activities such as commercial fisheries, oil and gas exploration and development, transportation, and tourism within and off-shore of Alaska."[14] Since there is no indication anywhere that tourism and fishing are or will be affecting polar bear survival, the governor in effect filed suit to protect Alaska's oil and gas industry from having to take any extra measures to avoid damaging the survival of a threatened species.

On more than one occasion, Governor Palin claimed that the Alaska Department of Fish and Game conducted a "comprehensive review" of the nine polar bear studies considered by the Department of the Interior in making their determination and that the state wildlife officials found "no reason to support an endangered-species listing." However, a later release of some internal e-mails written by Robert J. Small, head of the marine mammals program for the Alaska Department of Fish and Game, and two other marine mammal biologists, all of whom reviewed the research that the federal government was citing to justify a threatened-species listing for the bears, revealed that they had reached a much different conclusion: "Overall, we believe that the methods and analytical approaches used to examine the currently available information supports the primary conclusions and inferences stated in these 9 reports."[15]

Adding insult to injury, on August 12, 2008, with less than five months before President Bush left office, Secretary Kempthorne proposed sweeping and unprecedented changes that would further undermine endangered species protection. These misdirected rules shifted critical decision-making authority to federal "action agencies" to decide whether any project that they are advancing creates harm to endangered fish, wildlife, and plants.

On December 11, 2008, in a hastily arranged conference call announcing the new rules, a sheepish and awkward Fish and Wildlife Service director, Dale Hall, defended an outrageous evisceration of the agency's authority. Hall marginalized the value of his team of scientists, who have been giving their input on such decisions for thirty-five years. Director Hall was forced to preside over the crippling of the only two agencies with a wildlife and fisheries conservation mission. Rather than resigning in protest, Hall undercut the historic mission of the US Fish and Wildlife Service and National Oceanic and Atmospheric Administration's National Marine Fisheries Service, discounted the work of his own professional employees, and failed to stand firm for fish and wildlife.

The Bush administration, in this single stroke, did what special interests and conservatives in Congress have been trying to do for more than a decade: gut the Endangered Species Act. Fortunately, this retreat in the nation's longstanding commitment to conserve its wildlife was short-lived. Soon after the new rules were announced, the NWF, twelve of its affiliates, and numerous other conservation organizations launched litigation to block them.

In April 2009, the Obama administration fulfilled a campaign promise by reinstating the Endangered Species Act's requirement that federal agencies consult with independent scientists at the US Fish and Wildlife Service and the National Oceanic and Atmospheric Administration to determine if their actions might harm threatened and endangered species. However, they left stand the Bush administration's policy decision not to use the endangered species act directly to address threats from global warming.

Perhaps the Bush administration did the conservation movement a favor by providing a reminder of the fragility and crucial importance of our bedrock environmental laws. A broad swath of Americans immediately stepped into action. The public outcry against the misdirected and unnecessary provisions was phenomenal, with more than one hundred thousand citizens submitting comments opposing the changes despite the short deadline and the rejection of all e-mail comments. The public recognized that with these new rules, various pork-barrel energy projects, dams, highways, bridges to nowhere, and other ecologically destructive projects would have clear sailing past any serious outside oversight. Scientific experts' judgements of the impacts on fish and wildlife and guiding mitigation measures would be ravaged by ill-advised, destructive energy projects that add to the climate crisis. Putting the fox in charge of guarding the hen house has never worked before, yet the administration was determined to give it another try.

As government processes were failing the polar bears, the business world was failing them too. Ripe with the same shortsighted thinking that got us into this precarious climate situation, international oil oligopolies and their circumpolar sponsors saw the ice melt as an emerging opportunity to drill for more oil.

Watching the unprecedented Arctic melt of 2007, the Russians started the race by planting their flag on the North Pole seabed, angering the four other Arctic coastal countries.

They were not mad or worried about the planetary ecological threat but about the Russian oil development claims. On August 27, 2008, on the eve of a call for federal elections, Canada's conservative prime minister, Stephen Harper, visited the Arctic Ocean hamlet of Tuktoyaktuk and asserted Canada's sovereignty over a half-million square miles of the Arctic Ocean in order to garner oil industry support. Harper's far-reaching territorial claim dramatically enlarges the portions of the Arctic considered Canadian waters for the purpose of energy exploration and navigation, particularly through the emerging Northwest Passage. Harper's announcement fueled circumpolar regional tensions, as no other country recognizes this historically icebound passage.

The countries sharing the Arctic coast include Canada, Denmark, Norway, Russia, and the United States. They had a meeting in Ilulissat, Greenland, in May 2008, not to determine how they would work together to protect polar bears, Arctic fish populations, and other shared wildlife resources, but to carve up oil and gas rights in an ice-free Arctic Ocean. All are hoping the warming Arctic will yield up to one-quarter of the world's undiscovered oil and gas reserves. In this time of mass myopia, it is all about who gets to control the oil in the open Arctic ocean. Oil interests in the Arctic have more political influence than polar bears.

Look ahead with me to when the Arctic Ocean is ice-free. Affecting all of life there, climate change and its far-reaching consequences will define the future of polar bears and countless other species on the planet. Time is running out. Unfortunately, the bear's struggle to survive is just the tip of a shrinking iceberg. As the earth warms rapidly, more northward-migrating wildlife species will crowd into an ever-narrowing habitat bounded to the north by the Arctic Ocean. The fate of the Arctic ice becomes not just the fate of polar bears and other wildlife, but the fate of our children, too. By saving ice for polar bears, we may just save the known world.

Polar Bears Are Worrisome Indicator

Global warming is not just about the loss of polar bears; all Arctic marine mammals dependent upon permanent sea ice are at risk. Polar bears are just one of the worrisome indicators of the nonlinear shifts that are happening in the North Country. At the alarming rate the Arctic is now melting, the urgency and importance of confronting the climate crisis could not be more obvious. The US Fish and Wildlife Service was overly optimistic in its assessment suggesting that surviving populations of polar bears will be about a third of current numbers by 2050. Even though they still number about twenty thousand to twenty-five thousand worldwide, with about five thousand bears in Alaska, polar bears are in grave danger because of unprecedented habitat decline in the past two years as well as projected Arctic melt. Polar bears are our northern sentinels, and they symbolize the enormous threat of global warming to all of nature and all of humanity.

Scientists estimate that summer Arctic sea ice has about an 80 percent likelihood of disappearing in the late summer season sometime during the next ten years, and a complete melt-out may occur as early as 2013. As we approach that time frame, one question should be, Do bears deserve more than the limited "threatened" status? Does the polar bear merit an "endangered" status rather than threatened?[16] Andrew E.

Derocher asserts that the polar bear will be extinct within a hundred years: "You don't have to be a polar scientist to see that if you take away all the sea ice, you don't have polar bears any more."

Chapter 5

THE GREATEST SHOW ON EARTH

Some moments are so powerfully burned into our memories that they live in vivid detail for decades unscathed. When I was twelve, my grandmother took me to the famed Ringling Bros. and Barnum & Bailey circus. Long promoted as the "Greatest Show on Earth," the traveling circus was no longer under the big top, but had become an indoor event held at the newly opened Pittsburgh Civic Arena. I listened intently with sweaty hands as the ringmaster warned the nearly twelve thousand circus-goers to be completely silent because the "death-defying" flying trapeze act we were about to witness had never before been performed with the safety nets removed. The ringmaster explained that this feat required enormous strength, complete concentration, and utmost precision. One distracting noise from the audience could kill the daring young trapeze artists.

Barely breathing, we watched as they soared high above us. Back and forth on opposing swings, the two young performers were synchronizing their timing. The crowd gasped as one of the trapeze artists let go of her swing and spun through the air. In a split second, she was snagged from a rapid descent by her fellow performer, who arrived open-handed at that perfect moment. We collectively gasped again as the artist returned to her swing.

Imagine not one pair of flying trapeze artists soaring through the air; rather, envision tens of thousands, perhaps millions upon millions of them, all over the planet, every minute. Only then do we have an adequate metaphor for the elements of nature, which, like high-flying circus acts, are entwined in life or death harmony with other elements, all maintained in perfect timing. The difference is that for wildlife, their survival never has a safety net, and is dependent on finding food, shelter, and water at the right moments.

Where I grew up, great horned owls start their courtship during the last couple of weeks in December, and they incubate eggs in all kinds of nasty weather throughout the dead of winter. All of this hardship is endured to produce a pair of hungry fledglings at just the moment when rabbits and other prey species are producing an abundance of unsuspecting young. Synchronized in sometimes little-understood ways, harmonious links like this one have long fascinated amateur naturalists and trained ecologists alike. Various studies have shown the importance of physiological, genetic, and external stimuli triggering buds to break open, flowers to bloom, and birds to migrate. Various triggers regulate these fragile relationships, including photoperiod (length of day), rainfall, temperature, or a combination of these and other factors. So many different triggers, yet all of life has harmonized in a seemingly coordinated fashion to carry on for millennia.

Similar groups of species tend to respond to similar triggers. For example, many plants are triggered to emerge in the spring, primarily by rising temperatures. Many insect species also respond primarily to temperature. With global warming, many species are blooming and emerging earlier in the spring. In contrast, increasing day length, among other less influential triggers, powerfully influences many birds to migrate and breed. Because each trigger responds differently to global warming, it follows that global warming can dislodge and interrupt the synchrony between interacting species. Scientists studying biological responses to climate shifts warn that species will move independent of each other, not as "coherent communities," in response to changes. All of this will take place as the change in "mean global temperature alone will be one of the most rapid ever experienced on earth."[1] Varying shifts in ocean and atmospheric temperatures combined with sea-level rise could decouple many critical linkages in nature.

HORSESHOE CRABS AS A CRUCIAL PIT STOP

An extraordinary example of the intertwined life histories of different species takes place in Delaware Bay, the world's largest spawning ground for horseshoe crabs. Every year in May and June, horseshoe crabs swarm into backwater beaches along bays and coves and various partially surf-protected beaches in the Delaware Bay and Chesapeake Bay region.[2] Perhaps triggered by lengthening daylight or phases of the moon, horseshoe crab spawning occurs at night and generally peaks at high tides during the full and new moons. As they have for about 250 million years,[3] female horseshoe crabs return to protected estuarine beaches on successive tides, laying four to five clutches of eggs during each tidal landing, totaling about eighty thousand eggs each season.[4]

The annual horseshoe crab egg laying is an important event for hundreds of thousands of shorebirds, including dunlins, red knots, ruddy turnstones, sanderlings, semi-palmated sandpipers, short-billed dowitchers, and several other migratory shorebird species. All are attracted to a narrow band of beaches covered with millions upon millions of horseshoe crab eggs. If these birds are to survive the rigors of their long-distance migrations, their timing must be just right to enable them to refuel on the abundance of horseshoe crab eggs. The importance of this annual event is apparent when one realizes that large flocks of red knots gather along the Delaware Bay each spring during their long-distance migration. Incredibly, red knots migrate ninety-three hundred miles or more, from Tierra del Fuego in southern Argentina all the way to the Arctic. After nearly doubling their weight by refueling on horseshoe crab eggs in Delaware Bay, they continue their northward migration to their Arctic breeding grounds.[5]

This annual spectacle has provided millions of bird-watchers with one of the greatest shows in the natural world as the life of primitive ocean-roaming horseshoe crabs connects for a brief moment in time with the longest-distance air travelers. Thus, the perfect timing of migrations is a fragile thread in the web of life or death. Who can predict how climate change will alter these relationships? Anticipated sea-level rise can also make the difference between having protected beaches and not having beaches for the horseshoe crabs. What will happen to the crab eggs and the millions of shorebirds that seek them when these once-protected backwater beaches are completely flooded from rapid sea-level rise?

Citizen science has provided a treasure trove of data on bird populations and movements. For many years, the National Audubon Society and its local chapters have conducted Christmas bird counts involving thirty thousand volunteer observers. It turns out that bird migration patterns are changing as the climate changes. A recent assessment of the data gathered over four decades revealed that 58 percent of the 305 species tracked have shifted their winter ranges. According to the report, "Of the 305 species in the analysis, 177 showed a significant shift north and 79 showed a significant shift south. Overall, the average latitudinal center of abundance significantly shifted to the north by a distance of 34.8 miles." Some birds have traveled two hundred to three hundred miles beyond their traditional boundaries. The range of the purple finch, for example, has moved northward more than four hundred miles in four decades.[6]

THE PLIGHT OF SEA TURTLES

While visiting the John Day Fossil Beds National Monument in Oregon with my family, I was struck by the fossils of ancient turtles, which look nearly identical to modern sea turtles. Largely unchanged through millions of years, sea turtles have what paleontologists call "conservative evolutionary history."[7] While sea turtles have survived through many climatic changes over the past 120 million years, they are, by nature, slow to change themselves.[8] Seemingly as persistent as cockroaches, turtles have outlived their onetime associates, the dinosaurs. In light of this, some may think that turtles are built tough enough to last, to survive almost anything humans could throw at them, including abrupt climatic changes. After all, as the story goes, even the common box turtle can eat the deadly amanita mushroom, which would kill any mammal, with no ill effect.

Once well adapted to the tropical and subtropical ocean environment, six of the seven species of sea turtles are now listed under the Endangered Species Act. The six species in the United States are all threatened or endangered and include the green, hawksbill, Kemp's ridley, leatherback, loggerhead, and olive ridley sea turtles.[9]

Despite their persistence in existing for millions of years, sea turtles have been rapidly pushed toward extinction by a host of human-related impacts. Commercial fishing activities have been particularly lethal. Longline fishing, wherein baited hooks are laid out at intervals on lines often miles long, is commonly used to catch swordfish and certain species of tuna. Thousands of endangered sea turtles are killed every year by drowning when caught on long lines or from injuries sustained when caught and released from long lines. One study estimated that more than one hundred sea turtles are killed every year just in Hawaii's longline fishing industry.[10] Another source on sea turtles cites an average of more than seven hundred sea turtles of various species killed by longline fishing every year.[11]

Fishing nets are also lethal, killing sea turtles when their large flippers become entangled in open-ocean gill nets and they are unable to get to the surface for air. Shrimp-trawling nets also present a drowning risk for sea turtles. Despite efforts to improve fishing methods, sea turtle mortality in the fishing industry, called "incidental take," continues to be a problem.

Sea turtles spend at least part of their lives in coastal and estuarine waters, where the coastal environment is continually assaulted by toxins and other pollution. Toxic exposures in these polluted environments may be taking their toll on sea turtles. It was once commonly believed that turtles could take in organochlorines, metals, and other toxins with little effect. Environmental pathologists have long known that snapping turtles, for example, can accumulate large concentrations of toxins during their relatively long life span from feeding on species that bioamplify toxins in their tissues. Some turtles living near contaminated sites have been so loaded with organochlorine contaminants that the turtles themselves would qualify as toxic waste. As one example, back in 1985, Ward Stone, the well-known wildlife pathologist of the New York State Department of Environmental Conservation, found that snapping turtles were "highly contaminated with polychlorinated biphenyls, or PCBs." In his report, Stone described levels of PCBs in the turtles' tissues of 835 parts per million, which is seven to twenty-eight times higher than accepted government levels.[12] It turns out that while adult snapping turtles in heavily polluted waters can be highly contaminated by organochlorines and still survive, their offspring bear the brunt of the pollution. The young have a high incidence of birth defects including dwarfism, yolk sac enlargement, missing claws, and deformities of the tail, hind legs, head, eyes, scutes, and forelegs.[13]

Sea turtles have been less studied for toxins than snappers. However, a study led by Duke University in collaboration with the National Institute of Standards and Technology and others found that loggerhead sea turtles with higher concentrations of contaminants had poorer health. The study suggests that the sea turtles may be getting sick because of environmental exposure to toxic organic chemicals such as PCBs and pesticides.[14] Somehow surviving despite the pervasive impacts of incidental take and pollution, global warming could now deliver a knockout punch for sea turtles.

Like many species of crocodiles, alligators, and other turtles, sea turtles have what is known as "environmental" or "temperature-dependent" sex determination. Unlike sex determination by chromosomes, as in mammals and birds, the sex of these temperature-dependent species is determined by the temperature at which the egg is incubated during the first trimester. Below about 86°F, sea turtle hatchlings are male. Above about 86°F, they are female. Incubation temperatures above about 93°F are often fatal.[15] Even small beach-temperature increases could eventually lead to more females being hatched than males. With fewer males available for breeding, entire populations of sea turtles could be extinct within a few decades if we do not act to curb global warming.

Some scientists are suggesting that climate change has the potential to completely eliminate the production of male turtle offspring if mean global temperatures increase by about 7°F. They also warn that increases of a little less than 4°F could significantly alter sex ratios. Even if turtles can survive the effects that climate change may have on sex ratios, they will still have to contend with sea-level rise triggered by climate change, which would affect access to suitable nesting sites and critical habitats.

As geological records reveal, the long existence of sea turtles demonstrates that wildlife can be amazingly resilient.

But rising temperatures combined with habitat fragmentation, shoreline alterations, marsh subsidence, sea-level rise, pollution, and unrelenting fishing pressures may stress these amazing shelled reptiles beyond their survival capacity. Dwelling in an increasingly inhospitable marine and coastal environment with a rapidly warming climate, it remains to be seen whether sea turtles will survive even the next few decades.

SAGEBRUSH AND PRONGHORN ANTELOPE

For many of us, the vast semiarid West is largely defined by sagebrush steppe, the place "where the deer and the antelope play." After all, a significant portion of eleven western states is covered with sagebrush habitats, with Utah, Nevada, southern Idaho, eastern Oregon, western Montana, Wyoming, and Colorado providing substantial portions.[16]

In 2005, shock waves traveled quickly through the professional wildlife community at the 70th North American Wildlife and Natural Resources Conference when researchers from Oregon State University (OSU) and the US Forest Service (USFS) presented findings from their study that warned that up to 80 percent of the frost-hardy native sagebrush ecosystems will be replaced by woody vegetation and invasive grasses such as cheatgrass. Ronald Neilson, a professor of botany at OSU and an ecologist with the USFS, warned, "Increases in temperature due to global warming will be the driving force in these changes, along with less-predictable changes in the summer rainfall regime...Given the flat nature of much of this terrain, once the woody vegetation gets up and over the 2,000-foot elevation, it will be like opening the floodgates." The study suggests that the sagebrush of the Great Basin, one of the largest North American ecosystems, may contract to a small fraction of its current range when ecological changes that are already under way couple with expected climate shifts.

As the region continues to warm, frost-hardy sagebrush will be displaced by frost-sensitive species from the Southwest and other invasive species. The authors predict that frost-sensitive species, which are already moving north, will jump hundreds of miles farther north to displace the sagebrush. The authors further warn that the hottest climate scenario (which we are currently exceeding) "would reduce sagebrush to about 20 percent of its current area in the Great Basin, a fairly rapid change in hundreds of thousands of square miles of the American West." The study also suggests that "only a few small areas of sagebrush in southern Wyoming, the northern edge of the Snake River plateau, and small areas of Washington, Oregon and Nevada are expected to survive and persist under all scenarios."[17]

Similar research by the USGS predicts a 59 percent decline in big sagebrush habitat throughout the western United States with a doubling of CO_2 concentrations in the atmosphere from preindustrial levels, which will occur well before the end of this century if emissions continue to increase under business as usual.[18]

Meanwhile, pronghorn antelope populations have declined dramatically in the past twenty years. Leading pronghorn experts James D. Yoakum and Bart W. O'Gara found that continental pronghorn populations declined from about 1 million animals in 1984 to 670,000 in 1997. The Canadian population alone declined from 31,500 to 23,200 during the same period. In Montana, populations declined from 161,000 to 57,000, and Wyoming, the heart of the North American pronghorn population, saw numbers decline from 608,000 to 370,000 during this same time period. Clearly, pronghorn populations are under severe stress from habitat loss.[19] While excess coyote populations can, in certain situations, be a contributing factor, the loss of winter range is the principle reason for this decline.[20]

Climate change is coming to the West. The Southwest has been drying up, and the soil will soon be blowing away. The process of expanding desertification is already under way in parts of the Southwest, and it is subtly spreading northward. Poor grazing practices on both public and private rangeland fail to emulate the more resilient graze-rest patterns created by bison herds of the past. Heavily browsed sagebrush and overgrazed grasses are increasingly stressed. As the climate changes, species composition changes, and there are few native replacements. Inch by inch, drought-stressed soils are spreading, degrading, and eventually blowing away. Over time, soils will have less carbon and become progressively more sandy, gravelly, and rocky as organic matter disappears.

Arizona's Anderson Mesa was once home to the largest pronghorn population in the entire state. Unfortunately, loss of habitat integrity along with shifts in elk range have severely impacted this southern herd. But drought appears to be mainly responsible for the decline of the Anderson Mesa pronghorn population. A study of the effects of midsummer drought on pronghorn does "found that the number of doe pronghorn…seen on summer surveys in 3 areas in the Southwest was related to midsummer drought indices, and that annual variations in doe mortality might be more important in determining population levels in dry years than fawn recruitment."[21]

Many sagebrush steppe habitats have been fragmented by development or converted to farmland over the decades. Other sagebrush habitats have been severely overgrazed; improperly fenced to keep pronghorn out; invaded by highly flammable, invasive cheatgrass; and hammered by repeated fires. Degraded sagebrush habitats with reduced shrub and native bunchgrass cover are being invaded by exotic annual grasses and nonnative woody vegetation that have a greater tendency to burn and burn hotter. Increased temperatures, prolonged droughts, early snowmelts and elevated evapo-transpiration rates, poor grazing practices, and invasive species take a toll on fragile semiarid and arid habitats.[22]

There are many other examples of the decline in pronghorn populations across the West. An unpublished assessment of the Red Desert area of Wyoming commissioned by the National Wildlife Federation (NWF) documented a dramatic decline in the pronghorn population in the Red Desert area. Pronghorn declined from a high of about one hundred forty thousand in 1991 to about eighty-nine thousand in 2001. During the same period, total hunter harvest in the area declined from twenty-two thousand animals to two thousand two hundred. Clearly, pronghorn habitats are in decline and no longer able to provide for these historically large populations.

Global warming could tip an already fragile relationship between open, healthy sagebrush range and migrating pronghorn antelope. An NWF report titled "Fueling the Fire" summarized this increasing threat from global warming, saying,

"Any significant decline in the West's remaining native sage-brush habitats would have devastating consequences for sage grouse, mule deer, pronghorn and other species that depend on them."[23] Pronghorn antelope bouncing across open range symbolizes the West perhaps more than any other scene. Their continued survival is at stake as the climate warms.

MANAGING WILDLIFE IN SHIFTING ECOSYSTEMS

Wildlife habitats unencumbered by damaging human intrusions are inherently durable and sustainable. However, when humans overtake the landscapes' ability to renew itself, the habitats' resiliency is limited and rapidly reaches the breaking point for many species, not just polar bears, shorebirds, sea turtles, and pronghorn antelope.

Several published scientific studies warn that misdirected human activities are impoverishing ecosystems around the world and, when coupled with global warming, could lead to nearly a million extinctions by 2050.[24] Global warming is destined to cause rapid and large fluctuations in ecological conditions, triggering the loss of certain species for which suitable habitat conditions no longer exist. Sea-level rise and increased storminess, desertification, and other climate shifts will likely become dominant drivers of biodiversity loss and species extinction by midcentury. Couple this with the invasion of nonnative species, and the problem becomes even worse. At particular risk are many mammals, amphibians, plants, and reptiles that are already showing enormous signs of stress from other factors.

Changes in species distribution and phenological changes that disrupt the synchrony between species may also lead to significant changes in community composition and additional losses. In their introduction to *Climate Change and Biodiversity*, Tom Lovejoy and Lee Hannah warn, "In addition to the stresses that individual species may encounter in responding to climate, differential rates of response imply that current communities of species will be disaggregated...the consequences of the tearing apart of communities of species as now constituted are largely unknown."[25] Any and perhaps all of these predicted and unpredictable changes may alter core ecosystem functions upon which we all depend: clean water, clean air, food, shelter, and more. Reflecting on a time when the thermometer went up and rainfall disappeared, Donald Worster wrote a book entitled *Dust Bowl: The Southern Plains in the 1930s*. In revisiting a time when Nebraska hit 118 degrees, Iowa 115, and Illinois exceeded 100 degrees for so long that 370 people were killed, Worster observed, "Nothing that lives finds life easy under their severe skies."[26] As ecosystems collapse, nature will bat last, and it will take a mean swing on all of humanity.

As the Fourth Intergovernmental Panel on Climate Change (IPCC) report warns, we could easily lose about a million species if current CO_2 emissions continue and we fail to invest in adaptation.[27] For those who question the IPCC's stark warnings, numerous ecological studies and extensive climate modeling underpin these estimates. For example, a team of scientists led by Jay R. Malcolm of the University of Toronto looked at twenty-five areas of ecological richness, commonly called "biological hotspots," where 44 percent of the plants and 35 percent of the vertebrates on the planet reside on only 1 percent of the world's landmass. Their goal was to determine the potential for global warming to influence the future of these critical habitats and the species they hold. The key conclusion of this study was that tens of thousands of species could go extinct in coming decades because of global warming's drastic alteration of these critically important wildlife refuges that harbor vast biological riches, including many unique and at-risk plant and animal species.[28]

This study reinforces a study published in *Nature* in January 2004 by a team of ecologists looking at six large ecoregions. They predict that a doubling of CO_2 concentrations will lead to the extinction of 40 percent of species in some of the hotspots—a potential loss of some fifty-six thousand plants and three thousand seven hundred vertebrate species that don't occur elsewhere. Using IPCC climate models, one wildlife study led by Chris D. Thomas concluded that unless greenhouse gas emissions are cut significantly, somewhere between 15 and 37 percent of the living resources found in studied ecosystems will become extinct or well on the road to extinction by 2050.[29]

If you need further proof, with more than 93 million acres on 584 refuges and 37 wetland management districts, the National Wildlife Refuge System is the largest system of wildlife protection areas in the world. A recent report titled "Adaptation Options for Climate-Sensitive Ecosystems and Resources" takes data from this massive refuge system and concludes:

> Climate change will have [system-wide] effects on species and their habitats. Mean global temperature has risen rapidly during the past 50 years and is projected to continue increasing throughout the 21st century. Changes in precipitation, diurnal temperature

extremes, and cloudiness—as well as sea level rise—are some of the factors that are projected to accompany the warming. A coherent pattern of poleward and upward (elevation) shifts in species distributions, advances in phenology of plants, and changes in the timing of arrival of migrants on seasonal ranges in concert with recent climate warming has been well documented and is expected to have [system-wide] effects...

Projected sea level rise has substantial negative implications for 161 coastal refuges, particularly those surrounded by human developments or steep topography. Projected climate-related changes in plant communities are likely to alter habitat value for trust species on most refuges; e.g., grasslands and shrublands may become forested. Habitats for trust species at the southern limits of ecoregions and in the Arctic, as well as rare habitats of threatened or endangered species, are most likely to show climate-related changes.

The report summarizes many climate risks and makes an important recommendation that should be adopted into wildlife law and properly funded as part of our national climate policies: "A national plan should be developed to assess the projected shifts in biomes and develop optimal placement of refuge lands on a landscape that is likely to exist 100 or more years into the future."[30]

Clearly, the risks are high and increasing daily. We are the cause of this fast-approaching calamity, and we must be the solution. We have much to learn about these ancient rhythms and fragile relationships. A recent European Union report,

"The Economics of Ecosystems and Biodiversity," introduces the subject of biodiversity loss in an insightful way, knowing that most people today are more familiar with their computers than they are with the natural world: "Biological diversity represents the natural wealth of the Earth, and provides the basis for life and prosperity for the whole of mankind. However, biodiversity is currently vanishing at an alarming rate, all over the world. We are, so to speak, erasing nature's hard drive without even knowing what data it contains."[31]

CHAPTER 6

IN THE ABSENCE OF LIGHT

The heavens declare the glory of God; the skies proclaim the work of his hands.

—Psalms 19:1

A few years ago, we invited a group of low-income children from urban Pittsburgh to visit a distant natural area in Fayette County, Pennsylvania, for an owl watch. As night fell, the children became startled as they got their first glimpse of the myriad bright stars set in a clear, black sky. These kids had never seen a night sky in the absence of ambient light. Urban haze and light pollution had completely blocked their view of the heavens and dimmed their sense of the magnitude of creation.

Shallow news coverage causes most Americans to underestimate the urgency of the threat of global warming. Television's failure to adequately cover the climate threat, along with the deliberate opacity created by massive oil and coal advertising, masks the vivid realities of the situation, much like the haze and light pollution blocked out the reality of the night sky for those urban kids.

The television has been described as a weapon of mass distraction. On hearing about the methane leaking from the Siberian Sea, one Canadian blogger mockingly wrote, "Runaway climate change? Massive methane release off Siberia? Nah, let's talk about Wall Street instead!" Meanwhile, on "the upper decks of our 'Titanic,' everyone is worried stiff about a crisis on Wall Street."[1]

Denial is a too-common human tendency, especially around global warming. On June 23, 2008, twenty years since he first warned Congress that human activity was causing the earth to warm, James Hansen warned that a "wide gap has developed between what is understood about global warming by the relevant scientific communities and what is known by policymakers and the public."[2]

I have often wondered why so many media outlets have developed an excessive and endless fascination with fallen stars, kidnappings, rapes, and other violent crimes to the exclusion of news that we can actually use. Perhaps it is because Americans en masse watch that mindless stuff over and over again, thus supporting it and demanding more of it. Besides, that type of "news" is simple and cheap to produce and does not take a rocket scientist to present. Tabloid journalism, replayed continuously for days, weeks, and months on end, is apparently profitable. "Infotainment" is not journalism. Networks and cable channels focus on making news shows more entertaining to pump up ratings that link to greater advertising revenues. Nobel laureate and former vice president Al Gore described this in his book *The Assault on Reason* as "a new pattern of serial obsessions that periodically take over the airwaves for weeks at a time."[3]

Apart from the direct influence of coal and oil advertisers, I fail to understand why the news media ducks or ignores these terribly important stories. In September 2006, Katey Walter, leading a US–Russian team of scientists, published an important paper in *Nature* warning that melting permafrost in Siberia, covering more than 10 million square kilometers of Russia, is releasing five times the amount of methane previously estimated by scientists. Walter's findings equate the melting Siberian permafrost and the massive amounts of frozen methane that could be discharged to a ticking time bomb threatening the world's climate.[4]

You would think Walter's shocking findings would be newsworthy. Well, you would be wrong.[5] While Radio Free Europe, the British Broadcasting Corporation, and National Public Radio found it newsworthy, the mainstream US media was completely distracted by mindless pursuits. At this same time, network and cable channels were in a frenzy, with satellite trucks gathered in front of the Boulder, Colorado, district attorney's office to report titillating details of JonBenét Ramsey's warped admirer and supposed killer, John Mark Karr.

Another instance in a long line of US media failures occurred on December 12, 2007, when Wieslaw Maslowski, a research professor at the Naval Postgraduate School, told a large gathering at the American Geophysical Union meeting that the Arctic will be ice-free sometime during the summer of 2013.[6] Disappearing Arctic ice threatens to amplify global warming, yet Maslowski's troubling findings were not covered by any of the networks, not even CNN. Instead, US viewers were preoccupied with the strange behavior of Drew Peterson in the disappearance of his fourth wife, Stacy.

In an article titled "Dung on All Their Houses," Danny Schechter summarized the media this way: "Like the word processors found on every desk, there is an idea processor at work, narrowing down what future generations will come to know as the first draft of history. More and more, those stories revolve around some high profile "giga-event"—the O.J. Case, the Death of a Princess, Sex Scandal in the White House, a natural disaster, and so on. Like blackbirds in flight, packs of reporters darken the sky, moving in swarms at the same speed and in predictable trajectory. When one lands, they all land. When one leaves, they all leave."[7]

ADVERTISING AND NEWS CONTENT—CONNECTED?

In these recessionary times, the networks seem desperate for advertising, so it's not surprising that they will run just about any coal or oil ad no matter how outrageous it may be, because the fossil fuel industry spends so much on pure propaganda. To hide the truth about the industry, huge advertising budgets are used not for selling products but to mislead Americans. Today, coal and oil interests are spending hundreds of millions of dollars to saturate airwaves, television, and websites with advertisements designed to manipulate. Throughout the 2008 elections, the television media ran—almost nonstop—tons of opinion-distorting and flat-out-false advertisements from oil and coal companies and their fossil-fuel power generators.

The ubiquitous and misleading oil ads never disclose who the sponsors are—they just say "sponsored by API." Imagine the answers Jay Leno would get by asking people on the street to tell him who API is; few, if any, could guess that it is the

American Petroleum Institute. These commercial spots convincingly suggest that we have forty-five years of oil and gas left, yet the same ads say that Big Oil is investing in alternative energy research, development, and deployment. They're betting that most people will buy that contradiction, and so far they've bet right. These oil advertisers also spawned the "Drill Baby Drill" campaign that dominated Republican rallies in 2008.

Some media executives have forgotten that the airwaves are commonwealth property belonging to all the people. In granting private use of the public estate, the Federal Communications Commission once required holders of broadcast licenses to present controversial issues of public importance in a manner that was honest, equitable, and balanced. For decades, a policy known as the Fairness Doctrine was a backstop protecting the airwaves from being captured by propagandists who bought airtime. During the Reagan administration, a systematic effort led primarily by conservatives was made to erode and eventually eliminate the long-held doctrine. With the Fairness Doctrine now gone, networks have no legal obligation to provide any meaningful rebuttal to propaganda, including mass-advertising campaigns.

The elimination of the Fairness Doctrine was one of the most devastating attacks on truth. Do not underestimate the powerful alignment of media owners and talk radio voices committed to keeping it from returning. If you do not believe we need to bring back the Fairness Doctrine, read the very words that ABC executives thought were too controversial to run on national television during the election season in 2008:[8]

The solution to our climate crisis seems simple. Repower America with wind and solar. End our dependence on foreign oil. A stronger economy. So why are we still stuck with dirty and expensive energy? Because big oil spends hundreds of millions of dollars to block clean energy. Lobbyists, ads, even scandals. All to increase their profits, while America suffers. Breaking big oil's lock on our government, now that's change. We're the American people and we approve this message.[9]

These are obviously outrageous, even dangerous words because they mention the millions of dollars flowing to the networks from false energy ads. In the spirit of full disclosure, the above-mentioned inflammatory ads came from the Alliance for Climate Protection (ACP), a tripartisan organization founded by a nonprofit, nonpartisan effort composed of Al Gore, four well-known Republicans, three prominent Democrats, and one lowly independent (me). The ACP submitted the above ad to ABC to have it aired on September 26 during *20/20*. We paid $85,000 for the airtime, but the morning the ad was to run, the network rejected it.

After the ad was refused, the then Alliance CEO, Cathy Zoi, complained in an e-mail to supporters and donors that ABC, CBS, and CNN aired numerous television spots for the oil and coal industry during the October 7 presidential debate, but ABC was refusing to air the Alliance ad. In an e-mail on October 8, Cathy alerted supporters, "Did you notice the ads after last night's presidential debate? ABC had Chevron. CBS had Exxon. CNN had the coal lobby. But you know what happened last week? ABC refused to run our Repower America ad—the ad that takes on this same oil and coal lobby."[10]

The 2008 debates, news, and convention coverage were universally sponsored by the energy industry. ExxonMobil, for example, sponsored the convention coverage of CNN and CBS. It is safe to say that Big Coal and Big Oil owned the advertising space around the 2008 elections coverage. Far too few climate and energy questions were asked during both the primary and general election debates. Those few that were asked by the moderator were not followed up on for needed details on position differences. Since energy was the driving issue at the time of both conventions, you would think news outlets would avoid both the appearance and actual conflict of interests. Imagine how Civil War–era history might have been altered if a wealthy class of slave-trading merchants had funded the newspaper coverage during the Republican National Convention at which Abraham Lincoln was chosen.

Polls show that climate concerns actually diminished during the advertising blitz, when gasoline prices soared. Advertising has created the false impression that the energy industry is doing a good job taking care of the threat of global warming at the same time published science is making it increasingly clear that the actual threats are dire. Clean coal exists only on television and in political promises. Beyond the ads, there is no such thing. Leading up to the 2008 elections, the coal industry spent many millions promoting mythical "clean coal" in television ads and at the political conventions. At the same time, it has fought the very climate security laws that would advance the technological development of clean coal. The industry has long known that mercury pollution, tiny respiratable sulfate particles, and global warming are very serious health and environmental problems; yet the industry has done everything possible to thwart pollution controls while whitewashing coal.

An international poll, conducted just before the December 2008 United Nations (UN) Climate Change Conference and funded by the financial institution HSBC, the Earthwatch Institute, and other groups, surveyed people in eleven countries (Australia, Brazil, Canada, China, France, Germany, India, Malaysia, Mexico, the United Kingdom, and the United States) and found that only 47 percent "were prepared to make personal lifestyle changes to reduce carbon emissions, down from 58 per cent last year...And only one in five respondents...said they'd spend extra money to reduce climate change, [which is] down from 28 per cent in 2007."[11]

"CLEAN COAL"—A DIRTY LITTLE SECRET

Listen to television ads that promote "clean coal" a thousand times over and you will soon begin to believe that clean coal actually exists. At least that is the aim of the $45 million propaganda campaign paid for by about forty coal and power companies euphemistically called the American Coalition for Clean Coal Electricity. The ubiquitous ads camouflage a morally outrageous situation in which continued burning of coal is harming our children's mental health and jeopardizing the future of much of life on earth as we know it.[12]

The truth is that coal, as a high-carbon fossil fuel, is one of the dirtiest energy sources on the planet. Coal pumps dangerous volumes of global warming pollution into our atmosphere and alarming quantities of toxins such as mercury into our air, land, and water. When coal was being formed millions of years ago, the earth had many active volcanoes spewing toxins, metals, and acid-forming sulfur from its core; these pollutants were deposited in the coal-forming peat beds. Coal typically contains some of the nastiest elements from the periodic table, including, but not limited to, arsenic, aluminum, boron, barium, beryllium, cadmium, copper, cobalt, fluorine, mercury, molybdenum, nickel, lead, antimony, selenium, tin, thorium, thallium, uranium, vanadium, and zinc.[13] These pollutants settled in high-carbon peat bogs that became coal beds.[14]

When coal is burned and ash accumulates, nearby populations are exposed to dangerous levels of pollution and radiation. A study titled "Radiological Impact of Airborne Effluents of Coal and Nuclear Plants" published in *Science* magazine concluded that Americans living near coal-fired power plants are exposed to higher radiation doses than those living near nuclear power plants that meet government regulations.[15] According to another study by the National Council on Radiation Protection and Measurements, the radiation exposure from coal plants may be one hundred times that emitted from nuclear plants.[16]

Mercury pollution, largely from coal burning, is ubiquitous, and because of it, we all carry elevated loads of mercury in our bodies. Fish from nearly every body of water on the planet have varying elevated levels of contamination, depending on how close they are to emissions. Dangerous mercury exposures from fish consumption are well documented in the scientific literature, but polluters have fought against stringent mercury regulations that require what is known as "best-available control technologies" for years while ignoring the mounting evidence that children and developing fetuses are highly susceptible to mercury's neurobiological effects. Jane Hightower, author of *Diagnosis: Mercury: Money, Politics & Poison* recently wrote that patients

> began showing up in my office with similar symptoms that included fatigue, hair loss, headache, muscle and joint pain, and various neurological ailments. My effort to solve this medical mystery, and discover the thread that united these people, has led to a decade-long investigation of one of the most toxic substances on the planet—methyl mercury—and a slowly growing realization that the U.S. government has taken woefully inadequate steps to safeguard Americans from this health threat...The common link among all these patients was a regular diet of fish—and an inordinately high level of mercury in their bodies. When they stopped eating fish, their mercury levels returned to normal, and nearly all reported that their symptoms disappeared.[17]

Direct exposure to mercury from burning coal may be causing an alarming increase in autism rates in children. A recent autism study conducted by Raymond F. Palmer, associate professor of family and community medicine at the University of Texas Health Science Center at San Antonio, Stephen Blanchard of Our Lady of the Lake University in San Antonio, and Robert Wood of the University of Texas Health Science Center at San Antonio connected the dots between autism and mercury pollution. The study looked at mercury releases from 39 coal-fired power plants and 56 industrial facilities and compared the mercury emissions to autism rates in 1,040 Texas school districts. This important study linked increased autism risks to the actual distances from mercury-belching coal-fired power plants and other mercury-releasing industrial sources and found the following:

- Autism prevalence is linked to mercury emissions and is reduced by 1 percent to 2 percent with each ten miles of distance from the pollution source.
- For every 1,000 pounds of mercury released by all industrial sources, there was a corresponding 2.6 percent increase in autism rates in the Texas school districts in 2002.
- For every 1,000 pounds of mercury released by power plants in 1998, there was a corresponding 3.7 percent increase in autism rates in Texas school districts in 2002.[18]

This is no small matter. One million to 1.5 million Americans now suffer from autism, and autism is now occurring once in every 150 births and costs Americans $90 billion annually. In ten years, the Autism Society of America projects annual costs to be around $200 billion to $400 billion. Autism is the fastest-growing developmental disability, annually increasing by 10 to 17 percent according to the Autism Society of America.[19] While the authors suggest additional studies, which should be done, we already know enough about mercury's harmful effects to overcome coal and utility interests and require mercury pollution control measures.

Wastes from coal burning are another threat. According to a 2006 National Research Council report titled "Managing Coal Combustion Residues in Mines," coal-fired power plants in the United States alone produce about 129 million tons of combustion residues every year—"enough to fill more than one million railroad coal cars."[20] Most of this highly toxic waste is stored in unstable lagoons like the one that recently ruptured in Tennessee, destroying nearby homes and disrupting an entire community.

Carbon capture and sequestration technology does not exist at a single coal-fired power plant in the United States, and it will never be created without an aggressive climate pollution law. Mercury pollution will not be controlled without proper enforcement of the Clean Air Act. The coal industry and its allies have vehemently opposed both of these potential solutions.[21] In light of the many concerns, Orwellian ads claiming the existence of clean coal are a devious and dangerous fallacy. Coal interests spend millions misleading Americans instead of actually eliminating carbon and mercury emissions and controlling other toxic pollutants that spew across our lands and waters from coal-fired boilers.

Clean coal ads are a scandal in the face of the truth. To counter the dishonesty on the airwaves, the Alliance for Climate Protection and several other organizations, including the National Wildlife Federation (NWF), formed the Reality Campaign to debunk the misleading clean-coal ads.[22] Because of the disinformation campaign blitzing our nation's airwaves, the public is failing to understand the urgency of the looming climate crisis or the outrageous dangers mercury poses to innocent children and fetuses.

It is time we unite to confront this dangerous propaganda in order to build a clean energy future and restore our nation's faltering economy, simultaneously. The next time you see one of these manipulative ads, go online and complain to the networks and cable channels that run this dangerous misinformation. Let's also tell Congress that it is time to clean up our energy supplies.

Papers Going Bankrupt, Journalists Being Cut

Journalism as practiced by many of America's great newspapers may be dying. Sound journalism ferrets out truth; studies peer-reviewed, published science; and seeks to understand the published science, striving to present it accurately while making it less pedantic and more persuasive. That is hard work. It takes skill and time, and is often expensive. And for newspapers, it seems to be a dying art. A media industry Listserv at www.newspaperdeathwatch.com is chronicling this fatal spiral.

With the deepest recession in decades, the year 2009 may be even more deadly to traditional media. All across the United States, once-great newspapers are declaring bankruptcy. In recent months, a large number of venerable papers such as the *Chicago Tribune*, *The Philadelphia Inquirer*, *The Baltimore Sun*, the *Philadelphia Daily News*, the *Los Angeles Times*, Minneapolis's *Star Tribune*, *The Miami Herald*, and many multicultural community-based papers like LA's *Wave* community newspaper have filed for bankruptcy protection or, in the case of the *Rocky Mountain News*, closed their doors forever. Victims of circulation collapse and declining advertising revenues, almost every newspaper has cut staff as more and more people turn to the Internet for information.

Bob Norman, a writer with the online *Miami New Times News*, wrote, "The loss of news is almost imperceptible; there's really no way to know what stories we might be missing when there's no one there to report it. The Shrinking Three [*The Palm Beach Post*, *Sun-Sentinel*, and *The Miami Herald*] have handed down nearly 1,000 buyouts and layoffs during the past couple of years, according to my estimate."[23]

For years, there have been many signs that the media is doing news on the cheap. A study by the Project for Excellence in Journalism, for example, found that nearly half of the news directors surveyed cited "not enough staff" as the number one obstacle to producing quality news.[24] Since that survey was completed, the media almost universally has cut many thousands more journalists.

Traditional newsgathering, the kind that once sold newspapers, is labor-intensive and no longer profitable. Little time or effort is spent on making sure the news reporters are examining the right issues, asking the right questions, or digging deeper. Gone is the Watergate era of journalists going on long-term assignments to ferret out the truth. This is in large part why well-funded, old-fashioned in-depth journalism is in steep decline on US airwaves and newsstands.

Those with professional journalistic values are troubled that the news is increasingly driven by marketing and budget considerations. It costs money to hire competent writers who can ask the right questions on a complicated issue such as global climate change and who can search widely for answers to be sure that what the oil and government flacks say, for example, is accurate. Others, perhaps intimidated by climate chemistry, do not even know how to begin asking good questions, and they often do not have the time to find the story. Competent but overloaded reporters are easily baffled in the climate space. Few understand the importance of questions like:

- Are your conclusions from a controlled study?
- Were the results statistically significant?
- Is your challenge based on speculation, theory, or peer-reviewed science?
- Has the study been published in a scientific journal?

Today, those who are left in the industry seem to be forced to dwell on the easy stories that keep going around and around, day after day after day. Like an old record stuck in a scratch groove, the television media is now using the same video clips repeatedly and replaying the same tired sex or violence stories. Radio stations that were once locally produced are now broadcast nationally and do not have the staff capacity to report local news, nor do they cover national news. Few listeners seem to care.

The Society of Professional Journalists believes that "public enlightenment is the forerunner of justice and the foundation of democracy."[25] If that is so, can justice or democracy be secure in a media world where public enlightenment has been supplanted by the superficial?

In a *National Wildlife* magazine editorial in April 2005, I called global warming "the greatest story never told," because it had been completely ignored or discounted by the media for decades.[26] Now that it is a more alarming story, it continues to be poorly explained to the public, perhaps because those in charge do not understand or believe the urgency themselves. Until about 2004, most of the media rarely wrote or covered global warming. When they did, oil-funded spin doctors were generally given equal billing with the legitimate scientists who were actually doing research and publishing.

Walter Cronkite's journalistic values are gone, and Glenn Beck's are in. Media observers have been tracking this trend with alarm. Most people get their news from television, where environmental science is almost nonexistent or, when it appears, insufficiently reported. Some suggest that television news in general is in a steady retreat from serious journalism in favor of making money for the small handful of conglomerates that own the stations. To do so, they are cutting news staff and blurring the line between mindless entertainment and hard news. CNN, for example, sponsored a Glenn Beck special called "Exposed: The Climate of Fear" on May 2, 2007. Beck stated upfront, "This is not a balanced look at global warming."[27] Beck's intentional opacity was extracted from oil-funded deniers and was nothing short of appalling. The media is largely failing in its duty to separate pseudoscience from the real thing.

Beyond legal obligations, the privilege of broadcasting news on publicly-owned airwaves once came laden with a profound sense of responsibility for covering news, wielding facts gathered through old-fashioned journalistic work, finding multiple credible sources, and putting information into context with great care. The once highly regarded practitioners of the airwaves offered their personal opinions as such, and for what they perceived to be the good of civil society. No more; the supposed shackles of the Fairness Doctrine have been thrown off, and our airwaves are the worse for it. For the sake of creating controversy, the media allows a scientist's peer-reviewed findings to be challenged by deniers (often funded by ExxonMobil) without even requiring credible published data to back up the critics' counterclaims. Mixed messages are generated not from any published scientific study but from unprincipled and unqualified scientists who in several cases did not disclose their Exxon funders, funders who channeled monies to them through a number of high-sounding, nonprofit organizations.

WEATHER REPORTS: FAILING TO COVER THE OBVIOUS

Weather reporters have long avoided discussing emerging and ever-strengthening environmental cofactors within their weather reports. They generally deny extreme weather events' connection to a changing climate. In a presentation given at the fall 2008 meeting of the American Geophysical Union, Hartmut Aumann shared the results of a study based on five years of data from the Atmospheric Infrared Sounder (AIRS) instrument on the National Aeronautics and Space Administration's Aqua satellite. The AIRS data were used to observe certain types of tropical clouds linked with severe storms, torrential rain, and hail. The study "found a strong correlation between the frequency of these clouds and seasonal variations in the average sea surface temperature of the tropical oceans...For every degree Centigrade (1.8 degrees Fahrenheit) increase in average ocean surface temperature, the team observed a 45-percent increase in the frequency of the very high clouds. At the present rate of global warming of 0.13 degrees Celsius (0.23 degrees Fahrenheit) per decade, the team inferred the frequency of these storms can be expected to increase by six percent per decade."[28]

Weather reporters never mention this study or the many other studies that point to more extreme weather and stronger hurricanes with greater intensity and duration.[29] Yet anyone who is paying attention to the weather across the planet can see what is happening.

This is not the first time weather reporters have failed to share important scientific findings that related to the weather. When the acidity of rainfall grew to unprecedented levels in the late 1980s (and even damaged car paints all across the country), weather reporters, with very few exceptions, were silent on this threat. They have also long avoided reporting air pollution episodes, preferring instead to refer to them as "hazy skies" until they were nearly forced to report on air quality using data produced by federally sanctioned air-monitoring stations. Sharon Begley of *Newsweek* recently wrote:

> It's almost a point of pride with climatologists. Whenever someplace is hit with a heat wave, drought, killer storm or other extreme weather, scientists trip over themselves to absolve global warming. No particular weather event, goes the mantra, can be blamed on something so general. Extreme weather occurred before humans began loading up the atmosphere with heat-trapping greenhouse gases such as carbon dioxide. So this storm or that heat wave could be the result of the same natural forces that prevailed 100 years ago—random movements of air masses, unlucky confluences of high- and low-pressure systems—rather than global warming. This pretense has worn thin. The frequency of downpours and heat waves, as well as the power of hurricanes, has increased

so dramatically that '100-year storms' are striking some areas once every 15 years, and other once rare events keep returning like a bad penny.[30]

The Weather Channel stood alone as the clarion voice of responsible reporting. It was willing to stand the heat and tell the truth about global warming. *Forecast Earth* was hosted by Natalie Allen with regular contributions from climate expert Heidi Cullen. Cullen, formerly with the National Center for Atmospheric Research and the International Research Institute for Climate Prediction before joining the Weather Channel, knows what she is talking about. Cullen has flinty courage in the face of mean-spirited distortions from Rush Limbaugh and ugly attacks from his band of global warming deniers. Undaunted, Cullen consistently brought depth, clarity, and sound scientific interpretation to her climate coverage. The Weather Channel was alone in providing regularly scheduled information and advice on the latest science and living green.

I was concerned that when NBC purchased the Weather Channel in mid-2008 it would dim this bright bulb.[31] I was right. In its first major shake-up since its purchase of the Weather Channel, NBC turned the lights out at *Forecast Earth*, firing the entire staff of the environmental unit. Ironically, this action took place during the middle of NBC's "Green Week" in November 2008, and it leaves open the question of how long the Weather Channel will still cover global warming.[32] In a note to Heidi Cullen, NWF's senior vice president for conservation and education, Jeremy Symons, said it best, "I am appalled to see that NBC gutted the Weather Channel's

Forecast Earth staff. I know you feared this given the merger and economics, but doing it during "green week" is sick and tone deaf. It also ends a revolutionary approach to both lead and satisfy public interest in green issues, and I think the network will be poorer for it in the long run." Limbaugh had a different response to the firings at the Weather Channel: "People don't want to be preached to on the Weather Channel about the way they live. Just tell me what the weather is going to be and shut up."[33]

NETWORK AND CABLE NEWS

It is true that a limited number of investors hold the major networks and cable news assets. Increasingly, they also own newspapers, often cornering the regional news markets.[34] Because of lax rules and a laissez-faire attitude at the Federal Communications Commission (FCC), those who hold the keys control the airwaves. The owners no longer need to be concerned about accountability or oversight unless Janet Jackson has another costume failure. The network owners and station managers are now all about making ratings, controlling news production costs, and generating quarterly earnings. Cost-cutting by every news agency has eliminated scores and scores of journalists. The loss of reporting staff has created a "McNews" approach. The lack of substance in the media is crippling America's ability as a society to stay informed.

The United States has lost twenty years in a fight to stave off catastrophic climate changes. Until the television media quits distracting us with junk entertainment masquerading as news, Americans will not wake up to the urgency and solvability of global warming. Without enlightenment, millions of people and the known natural world will perish. The cynic warns that we will never do anything about global warming until it interferes with our television reception. Let us prove them wrong.

WHAT YOU CAN DO: TALK BACK

We need to get the media attention we demand. You can help turn the tide by:

1. Start by thanking *Time* magazine, *The New York Times*, *The Washington Post*, Anderson Cooper, and others who provide climate coverage.
2. Challenge the electronic media to step it up by letting them know when something important is happening.
3. Complain to the FCC (http://esupport.fcc.gov/com plaints.htm) when news reporters present bias and uninformed opinions as facts.
4. Contact your member of Congress and demand that cable services make room for the BBC and other international news services to compete with domestic producers of irrelevant entertainment parading as news.
5. Demand that Congress restore the Fairness Doctrine to provide greater oversight to the publicly owned airwaves to ensure the media are operating fairly and in the public interest.

PART III

TIME FOR RENEWAL
AND IMMEDIATE ACTION

CHAPTER 7

RENEWING, RECHARGING, AND REBUILDING AMERICA

Ere many generations pass, our machinery will be driven by a power obtainable at any point of the universe. Throughout space there is energy. Is this energy static or kinetic? If static, our hopes are in vain; if kinetic—and this we know it is, for certain—then it is a mere question of time when men will succeed in attaching their machinery to the very wheelwork of nature.

—Inventor and futurist Nikola Tesla

The end of the carbon age is in view. The age that Tesla once imagined may be just beginning. Perhaps not in the way that he saw it, but by using wind, solar, tidal, current, and geothermal energy sources, we are attaching our machinery to the wheelworks of nature.

Americans deserve safer energy choices and a rational energy policy that eliminates CO_2 and other fossil fuel emissions from our skies. Most know that we must end our dangerous addiction to Middle Eastern oil controlled by dictators who hold the United States with disdain, but few Americans have fully grasped that we are running out of time to avoid a climate catastrophe. Since energy from the sun and wind are free, why do we continue to be addicted to expensive oil and dirty coal that are overheating our planet and cooling our economy?

We must now move quickly to purge carbon emissions from every aspect of our economy and deploy creative ways to help nature remove excess CO_2 from the atmosphere. The good news is that all of this vital work will create millions of high-tech and green-collar jobs in the United States, and it will spawn new corporations whose business model is green and black. The biggest impediment to realizing this dream continues to be overcoming the entrenched and dirty carbon industry and their allies, who are blinded, brainwashed, or too threatened to see the wondrous transformation ahead.

Energy Efficiency: Carbon Neutral Buildings for All

Improving energy efficiency in homes and every commercial and public building could be the single most important sector for clean energy investment. Greening every building in the United States could cut total energy use by about 40 percent and put millions of Americans back to work. And, doing so would completely eliminate greenhouse gases from the building sector.

There are many wonderful opportunities for participation in this energy transformation. Americans own 114 million residential structures[1] and over 4.7 million commercial buildings,[2] and these buildings use 72 percent of all electricity and 36 percent of all natural gas.[3] Large-scale building renovation projects targeting the most inefficient buildings in poor to moderate-income communities could dramatically reduce energy usage while creating millions of new jobs in poorer communities where jobs are in short supply. As Van Jones described in his book, *The Green Collar Economy: How One Solution Can Fix Our Two Biggest Problems*, a green economy will create a demand for trained green-collar workers. "That is good news for people who are being thrown out of work in the present recession. That is good news for people in urban and rural communities who are suffering from a chronic lack of work. That is good news for people returning home from Iraq and Afghanistan. That is good news for people returning home from prison, looking for a second chance."[4] Energy efficiency will make US industry more competitive. It will lower electric, gas, and oil bills for financially struggling homeowners and small businesses. Cutting consumers' utility bills helps homeowners keep their homes, because energy costs constitute the second largest monthly expense next to mortgage payments.

A well-known, innovative architect and wonderful friend of wildlife, Edward Mazria, issued a challenge "to rapidly transform the US and global building sector from being the major contributor of greenhouse gas emissions to be a central part of the solution to the global-warming crisis." Mazria says his goal is "to achieve a dramatic reduction in the global-warming-causing greenhouse gas emissions [from] the building sector by changing the way buildings and developments are planned, designed and constructed."[5] Mazria and his Architecture 2030 organization issued the 2030 Challenge in January 2006. Numerous allies including the US Conference of Mayors, American Institute of Architects, US Green Building Council, Leadership in Energy and Environmental Design, Royal Architecture Institute of Canada, International Council for Local Environmental Initiatives, World Business

Council for Sustainable Development, and the Union Internationale des Architectes have joined this cause and are working to implement its appropriate targets.[6]

Architecture 2030 is proposing energy conservation incentives for both commercial and residential structural renovations and new-building construction that will create millions of jobs and a federal program to restore our economy. Mazria explains:

> Renovation is not only weatherization, but also would include adding shading devices, moveable insulation over glazing, new and more efficient equipment, moving walls, building new walls, furring out existing walls with insulation, re-roofing and insulation (white roofs in the south), solar hot water heating, photovoltaics, micro-turbines, passive heating, cooling and ventilation systems and development scale renewable energy systems. Even if we triple the cost of renovation in our 30% more efficient residential case, the savings to the homeowner still adds up to a hefty sum, between $213.35 to $471.53 per month. We are talking here about big savings including money, energy, and green house gas emissions.[7]

Mazria is now promoting the climate bill to mandate efficiency goals and authorize incentives. In a recent e-mail he observed:

> We are achieving our mission by galvanizing both the building industry and the Nation to adopt and implement the 2030 Challenge, a global initiative stating that all new

buildings and major renovations reduce their fossil-fuel greenhouse gas-emitting consumption by 50% by 2010, incrementally increasing the reduction for new buildings to carbon neutral by 2030. Data from the U.S. Energy Information Administration illustrates that buildings are responsible for almost half (48%) of all greenhouse gas emissions annually. Seventy-six percent of all electricity generated by US power plants goes to supply the Building Sector. Therefore, immediate action in the Building Sector is essential if we are to avoid hazardous climate change.

Mazria is talking primarily about renovations and new construction, but he observed in further recent communications that

weatherization usually consists of caulking and weather-stripping, insulation, storm windows and doors, tightening up ductwork, upgrading and replacing parts in HVAC equipment. It is estimated that about +/- 5.5 million homes have been weatherized to date under a (chronically underfunded) US Department of Energy's Weatherization Assistance Program since 1976, or an average of about 172,000 homes per year. The maximum cost the federal government will pay for weatherization is about $2,900 per unit. If that (pace) were ramped up to 300,000 plus units per year, the cost to the federal government would be close to $1 billion per year. Weatherization will net on average a 12% to 32% energy savings. This helps save some energy and create some jobs but will not transform the Building Sector.[8]

Reid Detchon of the Energy Future Coalition and Bracken Hendricks with the Center for American Progress issued a paper reflecting that

> much attention has been given by policymakers to the need for incorporating energy efficiency into new buildings—but home and business owners need relief from volatile energy costs today. Energy retrofits reduce energy consumption in existing buildings. Technologies include insulation, energy efficient windows, high efficiency boilers and furnaces, high efficiency appliances, programmable thermostats, and compact fluorescent bulbs. Efficiency is by far the cheapest way of producing new energy supply—3 to 4 cents per kilowatt-hour for energy savings vs. 8 to 10 cents per kilowatt-hour for electricity from a new power plant. In California, a state with three decades of experience running efficiency programs, every dollar invested in energy efficiency has generated $2 of economic benefits.[9]

SEEKING A NEW AMERICAN TRANSPORTATION SYSTEM

In America, transportation means automobiles and trucks, not efficient high-speed trains, light-rail, subways, and freight trains, the main forms of transportation in Europe. For too many years, the highway lobby has won the battle to channel the bulk of transportation revenues from what was called "The Highway Trust Fund" toward more highway construction. In a land of ever-sprawling cities, we are desperately dependent on polluting foreign oil as a result of this undue influence.

President Barack Obama has become an outspoken

champion for a high-speed rail system. He is right about this. America needs to have high-speed rail that can be powered by wind and solar electric to interconnect every major city. Perhaps, through the reauthorization of the transportation laws, his administration can reform transportation policy and alter investment patterns that date back to President Eisenhower.

The auto industry actually lobbied aggressively against fuel-efficiency standards for years and continued to build gas-guzzling Hummers and other inefficient vehicles. All the while, American consumers continued to send billions to the Middle East to buy crude. In his 2009 budget message, President Obama acknowledged the "bad decisions," observing:

> As for our auto industry, everyone recognizes that years of bad decision-making and a global recession have pushed our automakers to the brink. We should not, and will not, protect them from their own bad practices. But we are committed to the goal of a re-tooled, re-imagined auto industry that can compete and win. Millions of jobs depend on it. Scores of communities depend on it. And I believe the nation that invented the automobile cannot walk away from it.
>
> None of this will come without cost, nor will it be easy. But this is America. We don't do what's easy. We do what is necessary to move this country forward.[10]

American auto manufacturers, long reluctant to create a new direction, now find themselves boxed in, not just by legacy inefficiencies, lack of a clear national energy policy, bad transportation policy, and a deep recession, but by the classic paradigm blindness that has hampered their transformation for decades. The industry has been steering by looking through their rearview mirror. Auto manufacturers suffer from a chronic institutional inability to see the future and a lack of resolve to reinvent the auto industry to fit that future. The entire industry became insular and disconnected from the dangerous realities of climate change and unstable foreign oil dependence, and completely insensitive to the changing political landscape.

No one illustrates this better than Robert A. Lutz, who was until February 17, 2009, General Motors's vice chairman of product development and chairman of GM North America operations. Lutz is well known for his outlandish comments on *Saturday Night Live* and for speaking his mind through his blog, no matter how little he may know about a given subject. During a private lunch with reporters in Virginia, Lutz said global warming "is a total crock of sh*t" and followed that up by saying, "I'm a skeptic, not a denier. Having said that, my opinion doesn't matter."[11] Actually, Lutz's attitude matters to tens of thousands of autoworkers who will lose their jobs because inefficient cars are no longer marketable auto designs. His opinions also matter to every American who has had to pick up the tab for GM's debts. Attitude matters to the future of the auto industry, and, oh yes, there is that other thing: it matters to life on the planet.

As GM was reorganizing in early 2009, Lutz said it was "a good time to retire" because he didn't want to have to "worry about that stuff," meaning new regulations and standards to improve energy efficiency.[12]

As a result of their need of federal bailout, GM developed a recovery plan, which was rejected by the Obama administration. One of the best elements of the rejected GM plan was a strategy to transform GM with electric cars that would be powered by wind, solar, geothermal, and other carbon-free energy sources.[13] At the time, the National Wildlife Federation (NWF) supported GM's commitment to battery-powered cars as a part of the bailout plan. On the eve of their bailout, GM's CEO, Rick Wagoner, pledged on a conference call with me and a couple of other environmental leaders to make the Volt a street-ready reality by 2010. I believe Wagoner was sincere in his efforts and I supported his focus on electric cars. Electric cars, if fully deployed, could be a vital link in a modern "smart grid," as their batteries can be used to buffer intermittent solar and wind sources while allowing for off-peak recharge, storage, and peak power-sharing. GM's OnStar in-vehicle security, communications, and diagnostics system could serve as a vital link to the smart grid to better manage car batteries as part of a distributed grid system.

Despite Wagoner's promise, GM's once heavily-touted Volt is at this stage highly uncertain. After rejecting GM's first plan, the Obama administration asked them to develop another plan with deeper cuts and, in a more controversial move, to fire their CEO, Rick Wagoner, which they did, in March 2009. Since Wagoner was forced out, the future of the Volt is uncertain. The new GM leadership has indicated that nothing is off the table as GM enters bankruptcy. It is not known if the direction toward cars that run on carbon-free sources will survive the next round of corporate cuts and bankruptcy court actions. For the sake of the many autoworkers, their families, and our planet, GM and the other automakers must make the tough changes ahead and move beyond fossil fuels to truly renewable energy sources through battery-powered cars.

In any case, the age of gasoline-powered cars must end, and it is not exactly clear which option will win out and replace our current, high-carbon system. Will our future be electric cars with batteries powered by wind, solar, and geo-thermal? Will future vehicles include carbon-negative biogas hybrids? (I, for one, hope that it is not based on corn or other biofuels that displace and reduce world food production or forests.) Will we break through the powerful highway lobby to build local electric light-rail and subways in every city and town? Will transportation be transformed to include a nationwide network of ultraefficient electric high-speed bullet trains, perhaps even the next generation of maglevs (monorail-trains that run on magnetic levitation)? If history is any guide, the future of transportation sadly may not emerge from paradigm-blinded Detroit, where change comes reluctantly and then only incrementally through federally mandated fuel-efficiency standards and subsidies.

Since the automobile of the future needs to be carbon-free, it is likely to be heavy on electronics and light on combustion. So future vehicles are more likely to emerge from Silicon Valley, from upstart companies like Tesla Motors. They have developed an "elegant electric roadster" capable of accelerations from 0 to 60 miles per hour in 3.9 seconds.

NWF's executive vice president and chief operating officer, Jaime Matyas, and I visited South African–born inventor and innovator Elon Musk, who is the chairman, product architect, and CEO of Tesla Motors. We met Musk at his SpaceX Company headquarters where he, under contract from the National Aeronautics and Space Administration, was developing what he describes as the world's most advanced rockets for satellite and human transportation. Musk is a wonderful twenty-first-century entrepreneur best known for cofounding PayPal and Zip2. He created a California-based solar company called Solar City so he could install rooftop solar panels that will provide energy to homes and recharge vehicles like the Tesla to give them a range of 40 miles per day without external energy inputs. With a full charge, the range extends to 220 miles (based on EPA combined city/highway cycle).[14]

The Tesla is powered by a 375-volt AC-induction air-cooled electric motor with variable frequency drive producing 248 peak horsepower and 276 feet per pounds of torque. This motor redlines at a whopping 14,000 revolutions per minute. The handmade roadster is powered by a 992-pound micropro-cessor-controlled lithium-ion battery with 6,831 individual cells supplying the juice. Most of the systems, including the power train, are managed by an advanced Power Electronics Module under direct software-control. According to Tesla's website,

> You'll see the hub of this network every time you pop the trunk—the Power Electronics Module (PEM). When you shift gears or accelerate in the Tesla Roadster, the PEM translates your commands into precisely timed voltages, telling the motor to respond with the proper speed and direction of rotation. The PEM also controls motor torque, charging, and regenerative braking, and it monitors things like the voltage delivered by the bat-tery, the speed of rotation of the motor, and the tem-peratures of the motor and power electronics.

When we set out to build a high-performance electric car, the biggest challenge was obvious from the start: the battery. Its complexities are clear: it's heavy, expensive, and offers limited power and range. Yet it has one quality that eclipses these disadvantages and motivated us to keep working tirelessly: it's clean.[15]

In the few days after Tesla's announcement of a coming family sedan, they had five hundred orders. However, despite the important technological advances, like its giant Detroit cousins, Tesla is challenged by the hard economic times, and so has sought $300 million in federal financial help. Three noted Silicon Valley capitalists have invested in Tesla, and the German auto manufacturer Daimler did in May 2009 what the US manufacturers failed to do. Daimler bought a 10 percent stake for about $50 million. I hope their commitments endure long enough to get Tesla Motors through the recession and into mass production of a highly efficient family car.

In January 2008, a second new car company entered the market. Rocky Mountain Institute, working with a consortium of visionary organizations including Alcoa, Duke Energy, Google.org, Johnson Controls, and the Turner Foundation, assembled an experienced team of hybrid-electric vehicle engineers and launched a new automotive vehicle company called Bright Automotive. Bright's first vehicle was designed and built in less than twelve months.

The first vehicle, designed as a van for fleet operations, will transport up to a one-ton payload and achieve one hundred miles per gallon. This van was also designed to serve as a family van or can be adapted as a taxi. This vehicle produces zero emissions for the first thirty miles while operating on a battery recharged by renewables. It supports the urgent goal of building a new energy economy by being a US concept that is built in the United States. An initial production run of fifty thousand vans per year would result in the creation of five thousand new jobs and, if successful, more will undoubtedly follow. (The current annual sales volume for delivery vans in the United States is over five hundred thousand vehicles per year.)

Urban Transportation Made Easy

In the summer of 2007 we crossed a threshold: now fully half of the world's population lives in urban regions. By 2020, it is expected that two-thirds of a much larger population will be urban based. So even if electric cars started rolling off the assembly lines tomorrow, it's still not going to make much of a dent in the huge environmental impact of urban transportation or alter the sprawling development patterns that the automobile engenders.

More needs to be done beyond innovative automobile propulsion to address urban mobility. The shift to sustainable transportation must be fundamental to protect the climate. Susan Zielinski, the creative managing director of SMART (Sustainable Mobility & Accessibility Research & Transformation), along with the University of Michigan's Center for Advancing Research and Solutions for Society, believes we are beginning to embrace a new vision for urban transportation that is clean, convenient, caring, and connected. The emerging, innovative approaches to sustainable transportation not only save millions of dollars wasted in gridlock, they are also socially equitable (accessible to all) and service oriented; that is, they cater to a range of needs by integrating various transport modes, new services and products, new technologies, and design. Zielinski reaches beyond those core essentials to suggest that the new generation of sustainable transportation is also becoming smart, meaning it is tech savvy, draws on various disciplines, and is sophisticated and sexy, conferring a certain status on users, and thereby supplanting the status that hot cars convey today.

There is more than a glimmer of hope at Ford Motor Company, the only American auto manufacturer that didn't need a bailout. Ford is shifting its attention to sustainable transportation. In June of 2008, Chairman Bill Ford announced their innovative approach to transportation, which actually begins to address the implications of a rapidly urbanizing, climate-changing world:

> This program will help make transportation more accessible, affordable, and sustainable in crowded urban areas. This is a very different approach not only for us but frankly for any automobile manufacturer...My great grandfather Henry Ford made vehicles affordable for the average person and in doing so he really changed people's lives—he changed where they could live, where they could vacation, and where they chose to play. [Ford Urban Mobility Networks] really reinterprets this legacy for the future. And that's why I'm so committed to it and so excited by it. It provides mobility for the average person globally and positions Ford again as the company dedicated to personal transportation.[16]

THE CHALLENGE OF BIOFUELS

In his 2007 State of the Union address, former president George W. Bush declared that the United States was addicted to foreign oil and pushed for the passage of the Energy Independence and Security Act of 2007. Bush's energy package mandated the production of 21 billion gallons of biofuels by 2022. As we warned at the time, corn-based ethanol expansion spawned by the act has been another misguided energy policy. Corn-based ethanol consumes as much or nearly as much energy as it produces and forces more forestlands and grasslands around the world to be converted to croplands. It also replaces shrinking food supplies. That conversion releases large volumes of CO_2 tied up in soils while destroying acres vital to nature's survival. One study found that corn-based ethanol "nearly doubles CO_2 emissions over 30 years and increases greenhouse gases for 167 years."[17] The same study shows that biofuels from switchgrass, if grown on US corn lands, could increase emissions by 50 percent if similar land conversions occur.

Of this total 21 billion gallon mandate (a mandate that only came about because of environmental lobbying), a portion is to eventually come from cellulosic sources (wood, grasses, or the nonedible parts of plants). Working with the US Department of Agriculture, the Environmental Protection Agency, and other federal agencies to develop sustainability standards for biofuels production, the Department of Energy has a research and development program to commercialize cellulosic biofuel technologies. The wholesale conversion of lands to produce cellulosic materials to create alcohol fuels is a mistake. However, if thoughtfully produced and carefully managed, biogas strategy may play a small part in our future if we can gasify corn stover, manure, wood chips, municipal wastes, and other organic residues to produce biogas, with biochar as a byproduct. By producing gas and biochar, biofuel production could actually be carbon negative and help pull CO_2 from the sky, locking it up in biochar that could be safely added to soil as an amendment. Meanwhile, biogas could power trucks and possibly be used as a long-distance fuel for electric-gas hybrid cars. Interestingly, no new technology is needed for this approach, as it uses all "off the shelf" existing technology.[18]

Another perk to this approach is that the biogasifiers (a device that cooks organic wastes into usable biogas) can be portable, cutting transportation costs by actually going to the fuel source in the forests or on the farm. The carbon-char produced as a byproduct of biogas could be deposited in the soils at the source, storing up to 30 percent of its carbon while creating a fuel source that actually takes carbon out of the air.

I am reminded of the hundreds of remnant charcoal sites that can still be located by their deep carbon-rich (carbon-char) soils. These Revolutionary War–period sites were created to fuel nearby iron furnaces that were once scattered throughout eastern forests. Now, hundreds of years later, significant carbon is still stored in the soil at each charcoal site, demonstrating the relative permanence of this form of carbon storage.

Realizing a National Smart Grid

Because much of the most viable wind and solar energy sources are far from major population (load) centers where the energy is needed, President Obama's stimulus package provides substantial funding to update the US power distribution system to a single green smart grid. The US electricity transmission and distribution system is not a singular system. It is a privately managed Byzantine collection of utility service territories linked together by high-voltage lines extending over one hundred fifty thousand miles. Configured into regional networks, the system is self-serving, antiquated, inefficient, and insufficiently interconnected. This largely one-way power line collection was configured in a piecemeal approach over the past one hundred years by many independent utility companies to deliver electricity, largely from dirty coal plants, to consumers. It transports electricity—with substantial and unnecessary transmission losses—mostly from carbon-polluting, coal-fired power plants to what are called load centers (businesses and consumers). Transmission losses often exceed 10 percent of total electricity generated, and the grid as configured simply does not serve future clean energy needs.

However, it is not all bad. Because there are few large sources of energy on the grid, the existing distribution has been relatively reliable and has little trouble serving current needs, but that formula will not work in a distributed energy environment. As hard as it may be to believe, our twenty-first-century US electric grid evolved almost haphazardly from late-nineteenth-century origins and remains insufficiently interconnected to facilitate future energy technologies or to provide opportunities for distributed energy production, two-way transmission between producing facilities, multiple storage capacities and using devices, and web-based smart metering, which gives consumers greater control and allows car batteries to be used more effectively.

Upgrading the grid could cut huge energy losses and would produce, according to the Department of Energy, "hundreds of millions of dollars in annual savings to the nation's electricity bill." The Department of Energy warned in 2002 that

> there is growing evidence that the US transmission system is in urgent need of modernization. The system has become congested because growth in electricity demand and investment in new generation facilities have not been matched by investment in new transmission facilities. Transmission problems have been compounded by the incomplete transition to fair and efficient competitive wholesale electricity markets. Because the existing transmission system was not designed to meet present demand, daily transmission constraints or "bottlenecks" increase electricity costs to consumers and increase the risk of blackouts.[19]

Each of the fifty states has its own complex and inaccessible set of public utility laws and rules that restrict access from distributed clean energy suppliers to the electric grid, and most state public utility commissions stifle innovation and consumer choice. State rules generally use disincentives to discourage or block users from efficient end-user cogeneration from sources such as solar and wind, preventing the grid from becoming a two-way pathway to move energy from a distributed generation system that would include homes and automobiles. If those archaic rules were preempted by a federal framework built along the lines of California's progressive approach, every American could turn his or her home into a solar or gas-fired cogeneration "power plant."

Though the Department of Energy identified some of the problems with the grid, a modernized "smart" transmission system is an urgent priority that has generally been neglected. The smart grid should connect solar energy capacity in the desert Southwest and wind energy capacity in the Midwest, to the faraway Northeast, and coastal load centers. By providing superconducting technology in a high-voltage underground direct-current backbone, electricity can be moved more efficiently over long distances to supply our homes and cars with energy. The build-out of the federally regulated grid should end piecemeal energy practices and preferentially serve up carbon-free energy, including techniques such as "least-carbon dispatch" of clean power. This means that transmission policy reforms must result in a smart grid that advances new clean renewable energy over old dirty sources to prevent the spread of polluting energy sources by ensuring that lines connect distant clean renewable energy to regional load centers.

The smart grid must also advance the considerable contributions that can emerge from community-based and so-called "distributed" solar, geothermal, and wind generation. Through efficiency, we need to make every effort to control waste and maximize existing transmission infrastructures by way of voltage upgrades and transmission service improvements. The grid should also give consumers smart metering tools that they need to detect and eliminate waste and better manage their demand and an ability to share distributed generation.

With sound planning, we can protect unique and sensitive

ecosystems, unbroken wildlife habitats, and cultural resources, as well as national parks and other protected public lands. With greater care, we can locate energy production facilities and the smart grid in places that do not sacrifice fragile wildlife habitats or damage America's landscape treasures. Regional, state, and federal wildlife and resource agencies must be engaged in transmission planning processes. In this context, federal policy should include several key elements, including careful planning for nationwide interconnections crucial to the development of a twenty-first-century grid that uses existing corridors to the fullest extent possible. Planners should utilize existing transmission corridors and other rights-of-way including existing pipelines, roads, and rail lines prior to encroaching on new lands. Power corridor planning should comply with environmental laws, including the National Environmental Policy Act. The siting process must also be open, fair, science-based, and provide for public involvement. Federal policies should reform and transform outdated inefficient state-controlled systems that favor dirty coal. California's "Renewable Energy Transmission Initiative" may be the best model for better planning.

A nationally coordinated, ultra-high-voltage transmission grid must be the backbone to a new energy future, and it must be built on a fast track to send that energy efficiently across the entire nation, giving every American access to solar and wind energy.

Carbon-free Energy

I like much of "A Solar Grand Plan," published in *Scientific American* in January 2008. Authors Ken Zweibel, James Mason, and Vasilis Fthenakis say that solar energy's potential is off the chart. The energy in sunlight striking the earth for 40 minutes is equivalent to global energy consumption for a year. The U.S. is lucky to be endowed with a vast resource; at least 250,000 square miles of land in the Southwest alone are suitable for constructing solar power plants, and that land receives more than 4,500 quadrillion British thermal units (Btu) of solar radiation a year. Converting only 2.5 percent of that radiation into electricity would match the nation's total energy consumption in 2006.

The authors further suggest that we must set aside huge tracts of southwestern desert lands to be "covered with photovoltaic panels and solar heating troughs…If wind, biomass, and geothermal sources were also developed, renewable energy could provide 100 percent of the nation's electricity and 90 percent of its energy by 2100." They also suggest that this clean energy can be produced and delivered competitively with dirty fuels such as coal and oil.[20] New energy developments must be planned creatively to avoid the most important ecological areas, and they must move quickly in order to implement clean energy solutions as soon as humanly possible. To accomplish such a grand plan for a clean energy future, energy planners must carefully screen and prioritize suitable areas for wind and solar while avoiding critical habitats, ecologically and culturally sensitive or protected areas and parks. Careful planning can identify areas with the most potential for renewable energy generation and with the least ecological footprint.

I received a letter from an avid fly fisherman and retired water quality manager who emphatically states, "I am opposed to these alternative energy sources because they create more harm than they mitigate." The writer goes on to argue that wind turbines "impact mountaintops, permanently. Access roads and power lines have to wind uphill to reach those clusters, further fragmenting largely inaccessible forests." The writer shares his belief in nuclear power, saying, "The environmentalists helped stop nuclear power development and it sure looks now like a bad call."[21]

While I am sympathetic to those who oppose this or any other power development on ecological grounds, let me suggest that we must use great care in siting such wind or solar projects to avoid the worst ecological consequences, but we cannot let encroachments on mountaintops or on the desert deter progress on ending CO_2 pollution. Those who oppose large-scale solar or wind projects do not understand the scale, pace, or urgency of the climate risks we face. No energy source—including the proposed offshore wind projects along the New England coast, biomass, mountaintop wind projects along the Appalachian mountain chain, numerous wind projects in the Midwest, or the solar projects suggested in the Southwest—will be perfect or without some ecological consequence. However, we must count the costs of failure to act and balance the alternatives. New energy developments must be planned creatively, and we must move quickly to implement clean energy solutions.

I lived through the early hours of the nation's worst nuclear accident, at Three-Mile Island, with its corporate cover-up and operator incompetence. I was in the Pennsylvania Capitol Building with Lt. Governor William Scranton III and the members of Governor Richard Thornburgh's Energy Council, who were seeking answers from an operator who was playing Russian roulette with millions of Pennsylvania residents' lives and lying to us. Later, while staffing the Select House Committee investigating the accident, I learned the graphic details of an incompetent and unqualified operator who cut the chains off the emergency core cooling system's gate valves with bolt cutters, thereby starving the reactor core of vital cooling water, and sent a brand-new reactor into a nearly full-blown meltdown.

Until recently, and for more than thirty years, the expensive debacle and near catastrophe at Three-Mile Island stopped all US investments in nuclear technology. The resurgence has been fueled by new nuclear designs and huge federal subsidies that help utilities pay for nuclear plants, which, "if completed, would be among the most expensive projects ever built in the country."[22] During the industry's down years in the United States, manufacturing moved offshore, so we no longer have the capacity to build nuclear plant vessels here.

Nonetheless, armed with generous federal subsidies, seventeen power companies are now proposing more than thirty new nuclear plants. Republicans in the Senate, under the leadership of Senator John McCain (AZ), Senator Lamar Alexander (TN), and Senator Lindsey Graham (SC), will probably require additional commitments to nuclear power as a part of any bipartisan climate bill and treaty. Ratifying any climate treaty will require sixty-seven votes in the Senate, and that means both Republican and Democratic votes will be needed, so we should not be surprised to see some nuclear provisions in any final bill. Additional nuclear power, even with this legislative push, will be of little help in the near term, as it takes more than a decade to get a nuclear plant designed, approved, built, and deployed.

For decades, oil, nuclear, and coal have enjoyed increasing preferential public policy treatment over energy efficiency, solar, advanced geothermal, and wind. In the $700 billion bailout enacted in 2008, for example, Congress gave Big Coal $25 billion in subsidies to liquefy a dirty fuel. Ironically, coal is receiving congressional largesse at a time when its future is rightly questioned by environmentalists.

Many in Congress have an outdated view of coal as a job maker. A recent *Fortune* magazine article by Todd Woody titled "Wind Jobs Outstrip Coal Mining" explains that

> wind industry jobs jumped to 85,000 in 2008, a 70% increase from the previous year, according to a report released from the American Wind Energy Association. In contrast, the coal industry employs about 81,000 workers. (...Coal employment has remained steady in recent years though it's down by nearly 50% since 1986.) Wind industry employment includes 13,000 manufacturing jobs concentrated in regions of the country hard hit by the deindustrialization of the past two decades.[23]

As part of the Bush-led bailout, Big Oil got an $800 million boost to advance oil shale technologies. With hundreds of billions of dollars in incentives flowing to the dirtiest sources of energy, there can be little wonder why we are having an energy market failure on a colossal scale.

For decades, enormous tax breaks and direct subsidies have flowed through influential lobbyists to the entrenched and powerful coal and oil interests they represent. US energy policy under the Bush administration continued to invest heavily in oil and coal through lavish tax breaks and direct subsidies and by not counting the true costs to society of fossil fuel pollution. Meanwhile, the oil industry wanted Congress to give them full possession of all remnant oil reserves and oil shale deposits, no matter how small or dirty they may be. In the face of exploding world oil demand, these companies make it clear that they will grab every barrel—offshore, in wildlife refuges, and anywhere else—regardless of how much damage it causes to fragile ecosystems and with no promise to deliver that oil to US markets anytime soon.[24]

For too long, the White House and Congress have become limited-access institutions where big money mattered most. According to a Center for Public Integrity analysis, there are now 2,340 lobbyists representing more than 770 companies and interest groups who revealed on their 2008 Senate disclosure forms that they are trying to influence federal policy on climate change.[25] While there may be a hundred or so religious, social, and environmental lobbyists who are counted in this number, the majority are from well-heeled polluting energy interests and K Street lobby shops representing special interests and their cronyism. These forces, along with childish and toxic political bickering, have blocked progress, wasted precious time, and distracted attention from the pressing realities of our changing world.

The root cause of the energy crisis is not lack of availability of alternative energy solutions but the absence of political leadership to overthrow oil and coal interests in favor of new energy and a new political pathway. Boise Penrose, an old-time political boss, once said that "politics is the art of taking money from the rich and votes from the poor, all under the pretext of protecting one from another." In the 2008 election, with millions of small online contributions to Barack Obama, Americans proved a new pathway to victory and to power. Lawmakers now must reject the influences of old money in favor of this new political formula.

Energy choices must be judged on whether they pollute the air with CO_2, mercury, and other toxic chemicals. Choices should also be considered according to whether the energy can be domestically produced by tapping abundant supplies, if it will provide good local jobs, and whether it offers consumers reasonably priced energy. On all accounts, national energy policy should advance renewable energy supplies over dirty fossil fuels. It is not possible to detail every opportunity in front of us, but it is important to say that capital requirements and political will aside, we have enough clean energy technology and efficiency potential today to cut carbon emissions to net zero in a decade or two. While the United States must fund research and development for new and unconventional approaches to energy generation, the technology to move forward is ready for use. Entrepreneurs have already invented many wonderful new pathways that, with a clear and strong market signal, will trigger a quantum leap in technology to a vibrant future. The political will is urgently required.

Research laboratories have assembled visionary inventors, engineers, and scientists. They need funding to help us to move to the next generation of carbon-free energy solutions. For example, many promising approaches may be found in the field of nanotechnology. Carbon-negative gasification using algae, duckweed, or even tobacco with biochar as a byproduct also holds promise as carbon-negative energy sources.

Maglev transportation and advanced geothermal (using the heat produced by in situ, low-level nuclear decay) all appear to be viable options needing careful consideration as we explore all carbon-free options. Meanwhile, efficiency, wind, solar (both large-scale thermal base-load solar and photovoltaics), ocean current–driven turbines, hydraulic tidal machines, and battery-powered cars are at or near our doorstep, and we must demand rapid deployment. They languish for lack of a pentalty price on carbon emissions, which would make them relatively more economical compared to carbon-intensive alternatives; insufficient funding; or lack of a level playing field. These are the unmistakable symptoms of the failed energy and transportation policies that currently give advantage to oil and coal interests over the interests of life on the planet.

AMERICA AT A CROSSROADS

In the fall of 2008, Americans voted for change, and change starts with energy, as President Obama said in different ways on several occasions on the campaign trail. President Obama has assembled an outstanding environmental and natural resource team. John P. Holdren, for example, now Obama's chief science advisor, has made it clear that "the world is already experiencing 'dangerous anthropogenic interference in the climate system.'" As professor of earth and planetary sciences at Harvard, Holdren wrote, "Global warming is a misnomer, because it implies something that is gradual, something that is uniform, something that is quite possibly benign. What we are experiencing with climate change is none of those things. It is certainly not uniform. It is rapid compared to the pace at which social systems and environmental systems can adjust. It is certainly not benign. We should be calling it 'global climatic disruption' rather than 'global warming.'"[26] Holdren; Carol Browner, Obama's "climate czar"; and the entire Obama team are the right people, but they desperately need our help to pass the right set of carbon-capping legislative policies to get the job done.

Ending two unfinished wars, repairing a fractured global economy, and dealing with so many other neglected matters in our world would be a distraction for any leader. But energy policy must take a front seat. Let us push for solutions at a pace and scale that match the magnitude and speed of the threat. Bold national policies that achieve real emissions reductions, workable international treaties forged in a spirit of cooperation, and a new understanding about sharing technology and financial resources are all essential elements to drive this transformation to every corner of the world. The world still looks to the United States to lead responsibly.

We need to advance solutions to America's greatest challenges—the economy, energy, and global warming—through comprehensive climate and energy legislation that caps carbon pollution. The United States can lead or be left behind in the clean energy revolution. We need to design and build advanced technologies here at home that the world will buy. We can continue to wait and watch as the impacts of global warming worsen and the costs of impacts increase, or we can act now to reduce the harm to our economy, our communities, and our natural resources. Congress can and must pass legislation in 2009 that gives Americans what they want: a clean energy future.

Congress cannot continue to support the failed energy policies of the past. The United States has barely survived eight years of a crisis in leadership, as it pertains to energy among other issues. The crisis was caused by special interests, by a failure to see what the future looks like. When will we understand that human existence as we have known it is only possible with a stable climate on planet earth? If ever there was a time to stop overheating the planet, it is now.

In his first month in office, President Obama worked with Democratic House and Senate members and three Republican senators to enact an economic stimulus package called the American Recovery and Reinvestment Act. The reinvestment portion of the recovery plan included $42 billion for transformative investments in efficiency and in new energy.

Congress allocated funds in the stimulus package to make a down payment on President Obama's campaign pledge to "weatherize at least one million low-income homes each year for the next decade, which can reduce energy usage across the economy and help moderate energy prices for all."[27] The administration should go far beyond the president's promise and adopt the achievable Architecture 2030 goals of making every structure highly energy-efficient by 2030. Through comprehensive climate legislation we should seek to set a ten-year goal of retrofitting 50 million homes and commercial buildings by 2020 using proven retrofit programs at the state and local level in order to cut the buildings' energy use in half.

On February 24, 2009, saying, "It begins with energy," President Obama gave his first budget message to Congress, urging them to invest

American Recovery and Reinvestment Act—
Clean Energy, Green Jobs*

Total Energy Funding	$41.9 billion	Notes
Fossil Energy and Carbon Capture	$3.4 billion	Investment in carbon capture technology research
Smart Grid and Transmission	$11 billion	Will facilitate new sustainable energy production; sound implementation is critical.
Total Energy Conservation and Renewables (not including transit)	$27.5 billion	65 percent of total energy funding
Energy Conservation Block Grants and State Energy Program	$6.3 billion	Adopted the stronger House requirements for the block grants and a higher funding level for the State Energy Program
Energy Grants (for schools, and loans for other Institutions)	$0	Funding for school energy conservation was cut in Congress.
Low-income Home Weatherization	$5 billion	This funding is aimed at achieving the president's goal of weatherizing 1 million homes per year.
Greening Federal Buildings	$4.5 billion	Greening of federal buildings will pay dividends in terms of future energy savings.
Retrofits of Public Housing	$250 million	This is the clean energy portion of the public housing upgrades.
Renewable and Efficiency R&D	$2.5 billion	Will fund advanced energy research to increase efficiency and advance renewable energy
Renewable Energy and Transmission Loan Guarantees	$6 billion	Conference adopted the better-written House language
Advanced Battery Manufacturing	$2 billion	Needed to advance intermittent wind and solar energy, and to power next-generation electric cars
Other (including clean vehicles, appliances, etc.)	$1 billion	Investments in efficiency
Mass Transit and Intercity Rail	$17.4 billion	The United States needs an electric-powered high-speed rail system.
Innovative Technology Loan Guarantees	$0	Taken out of the final deal

*National Wildlife Federation Legislative Summary

in the three areas that are absolutely critical to our economic future: energy, health care, and education. We know the country that harnesses the power of clean, renewable energy will lead the 21st century. And yet, it is China that has launched the largest effort in history to make their economy energy efficient. We invented solar technology, but we've fallen behind countries like Germany and Japan in producing it. New plug-in hybrids roll off our assembly lines, but they will run on batteries made in Korea. Well I do not accept a future where the jobs and industries of tomorrow take root beyond our borders—and I know you don't either. It is time for America to lead again.

Thanks to our recovery plan, we will double this nation's supply of renewable energy in the next three years. We have also made the largest investment in basic research funding in American history—an investment that will spur not only new discoveries in energy, but breakthroughs in medicine, science, and technology. We will soon lay down thousands of miles of power lines that can carry new energy to cities and towns across this country. And we will put Americans to work making our homes and buildings more efficient so that we can save billions of dollars on our energy bills.

But to truly transform our economy, protect our security, and save our planet from the ravages of climate change, we need to ultimately make clean, renewable energy the profitable kind of energy. So I ask this Congress to send me legislation that places a market-based cap on carbon pollution and drives the production of more renewable energy in America. And to support that innovation, we will invest fifteen billion dollars a year to develop technologies like wind power and solar power; advanced biofuels, clean coal, and more fuel-efficient cars and trucks built right here in America.[28]

We have barely survived at least three decades without a rational energy vision. That lack of vision is changing. On June 26, 2009, the House of Representatives passed the American Clean Energy and Security Act. The Senate is developing its own version, to be considered during the fall of 2009.

Our country also needs a new transportation policy to address future transportation needs and transform the transportation sector of our economy away from dirty, imported oil. This must not be delegated to Detroit automakers or Houston oil executives. It is time for our elected leaders to set transportation and energy policies that our children can live with. It is time to come together as Americans to demand bold initiatives grounded in science, prudence, and wisdom.

Regarding an international climate agreement, on April 5, 2009, President Obama promised a crowd gathered in front of a medieval Prague castle, "I pledge to you that in this global effort, the United States is now ready to lead." Obama also invited sixteen "major economies" to a forum to ensure that a United Nations pact on global warming is reached in Copenhagen in December 2009. At the forum, the president told the twenty-seven European Union leaders that "the United States will be an active partner in the Copenhagen process and beyond. We must not only reach an agreement among ourselves but also present a common approach that will bring other countries into the dialogue."[29]

President Obama is right. The United States must provide global leadership and set the pace for greater carbon reductions in the European Union. Combined, the United States and the European Union must set the pace for China, India, and the rest of the world, and they must follow by agreeing to deep cuts and avoiding new carbon emissions. If world leaders at the upcoming Copenhagen conference agree to launch an all-out effort to cut total carbon emissions to zero in the next ten years or so, the atmospheric CO_2 may not raise much above 400 parts per million.

During my high school years, I pumped gas and repaired cars at an auto service station. I have looked at thousands of dipsticks, and I can tell when an oil change is needed. Let me assure you, the United States is long overdue, desperately overdue, for an oil change.

WHAT YOU CAN DO: PUSH THE POLITICIANS

Seas will continue to rise and methane will continue to leak from the tundra long after we drastically cut greenhouse gases in the atmosphere, so we have no time to waste. In addition to carbon-capping legislation, there are important policies that must be enacted. You can help support the Obama administration's commitment to a new chapter in international climate policy by urging the administration and Congress to adopt a tight schedule to end CO_2 emissions and by urging them to support an international treaty to do the same worldwide. You can help put the pressure on by:

- Getting involved in letter and e-mail writing, phoning, and lobbying your member of Congress and your US senators to get them to acknowledge the growing insecurity of a destabilizing climate.

- Asking lawmakers to put aside political differences and the endless bickering that goes nowhere and to start moving toward clean domestic energy sources such as efficiency, wind, solar, and geothermal. If lawmakers can move in that direction, we will set a new course toward recharging the nation's economy while stopping climate change.

- Joining any of many good conservation or environmental organizations that are working to avoid a climate crisis and supporting their work. To find one that meets your expectations, Wikipedia provides a link to the many environmental and conservation groups at http://en.wikipedia.org/wiki/List_of_environmental_organisations.

- Using your social networking sites to encourage others to act. Start blogging about global warming and stay informed about the latest science and policy issues. Read my daily blogs posted at http://blogs.nwf.org/nwf_view to stay engaged on wildlife impacts, legislative and policy developments, and new climate science and to learn what people and organizations are doing to change the outcome.

- Drawing from and linking your blog posts to a number of reliable free sites, including the National Wildlife Federation (www.nwf.org/globalwarming), Daily Climate (www.dailyclimate.org), or Climate Debate Daily (http://climatedebatedaily.com). Or to get a steady feed of the latest science, sign up for the Climate Crisis Coalition daily feeds at info@climatecrisiscoalition.org. College and high school students may want to sign up with PowerShift 2009 (www.powershift09.org) and visit Climate Classroom at www.climateclassroom.org.

- Learn more about the impacts of international climate negotiations through the C-LEARN simulator at http://forio.com/simulation/climate-development/index.htm. C-LEARN is a simulator designed for climate communicators, educators, and leaders of international climate negotiations, and its primary purpose is to help users understand the long-term climate effects (CO_2 concentrations, global temperature, sea-level rise) of various customized actions to reduce fossil fuel emissions, reduce deforestation, and grow more trees. You can ask multiple, customized "what if" questions and understand why the system reacts as it does. The Climate Interactive website, www.climateinteractive.org, has updated content for C-LEARN, including new front ends for the simulation and teaching and learning tools.

CHAPTER 8

PUTTING THE BLACK BACK IN OUR SOILS

Shaking hands with the new county agent, the old farmer scrutinizes his youthful, fair complexion, his suit and tie. The farmer's inspecting gaze and skeptical expression intimidate the young man, who is trying to make a good first impression. After a brief and fumbling introduction, the young agent waits for a response from the farmer. With husky, calloused hands grabbing the straps of his denim coveralls, the old farmer leans toward the young agent and braces him with a question: "Is my soil living or dead?" The young agent stutters a bit, wondering what the old man is driving at. "Well, it depends what you mean by living. Why do you want to know?" "Your answer will tell me a lot about what you know about soil and how you would treat the land," the old man retorts.

As the old farmer's question indicates, our attitude about the life-giving nature of healthy soil is a good indicator of how we treat our land. A fistful of healthy soil may have millions upon millions of living organisms churning about doing their work unseen and unheralded. In effect, the farmer is pressing the agent to see if he understands regenerative agriculture. Farmers practicing regenerative agriculture see soil as a medium endowed with myriad living organisms: viruses, bacteria, protozoa, nematodes, fungi, molds, pollen spores, weed seeds, slugs, earthworms, ants, grubs, shrews, moles, groundhogs, and countless insects, spiders, and mites, all doing their part to make soil thrive.

These farmers recognize the importance of abundant organic matter (about half of which is carbon by weight) and the special role organic matter plays in improving soil's tilth and moderating shrink-swell problems related to soils with high clay or mineral content. They know that sandy soils lose organic matter quickly and can become windblown deserts. They know that the organic matter content of the soil affects its texture, structure, drainage, permeability, and nutrient availability, and even the toxicity of pesticide residues. They believe a key attribute of soil is its ability to support diverse biological activity, and they do not try to destroy all competing life-forms. Rather, they attempt to manage such rivals down to acceptable levels using integrated and biological measures to avoid the unnecessary secondary environmental consequences of agrochemicals.

Many practicing commercial agriculturists whose methods are chemically based have treated soil as an inert substrate for growing crops. They see soil merely as a stratified physical-chemical mixture of sand, silt, and clay that they chemically treat to force greater crop production. Liberal doses of herbicides, fungicides, insecticides, and rodenticides are periodically applied to keep it that way.

Heavy, carbon-depleted soils must be regularly stirred to allow for minimal water penetration. The resulting exposed mineral soil is easily eroded. Each spring, tilling by tractor loosens compacted soils. Commercial farmers rely on powerful machines driven by fossil fuels to break up compaction in structurally damaged soil, and they depend on chemical fertilizers to replace nutrients that were volatized into the air or washed away from hardened soils by ever-intensifying storms.

It is easy to identify mismanaged farms in the winter months because of the drifting, dirty snow. When the soil is not held in place by vegetative covering, it is exposed to the forces of wind and water erosion. These commercial farmers give little thought to what is happening below the surface of the soil or to its life-giving properties. In semiarid regions, land that is mismanaged depends on heavy doses of irrigation water, often elevating soil salinity and water shortages elsewhere. Evidence that poor agricultural trends such as this continue can be seen in farmers' ever-growing reliance on agrochemicals and irrigation water and a peaking of soil productivity. US pesticide use continues to hit new records each year. Most chemicals are used to kill weeds and all pests, with little regard to the value of insects that pollinate crops and other forms of life that may help retain and improve soil tilth and increase carbon capture.

Particularly alarming is the attendant loss of organic matter in many soils. By continuing to rely on farming practices that deplete organic content by removing crop residues from fields and through increasingly heavy dependence on herbicides, this trend will ultimately deprive the soil of much of its ability to replenish soil carbon necessary to retain moisture, therefore also increasing its erodability. Increased use of chemical fertilizers, certain higher-yield plant varieties, irrigation water, herbicides, and pesticides have compensated for basic declines in soil conditions worldwide. Dependence on such measures will continue to mask the gradual carbon loss, erosion, and deterioration of the soil structure, hiding the food security threat for another day and perhaps another generation. Those who treat soil as though it has no life ultimately prove their case by destroying the soil's life-giving habitat by forcing it to give up its stores of carbon.

Recent research findings published in *Nature Geoscience* warn that as global warming warms the soils, it speeds up natural organic-matter decomposition processes. Myrna J. Simpson, associate professor of environmental chemistry at the University of Toronto at Scarborough, said, "Natural processes of decomposition of soil organic matter provide plants and microbes with the energy source and water they need to grow, and carbon is released into the atmosphere as a by-product of this process." Warming temperatures are expected to speed up the amount of CO_2 that is transferred to the atmosphere. Simpson adds, "Soil contains more than twice the amount of carbon than does the atmosphere, yet, until now, scientists haven't examined this significant carbon pool closely. Through our research, we've sought to determine what soils are made up of at the molecular level and whether this composition will change in a warmer world."[1]

Organic matter on the soil surface acts as an insulator that moderates soil temperatures, which are critical in a warming world, as studies have shown greater carbon leakage occurs in warmer soils. Healthy soil is loaded with organic matter. Organic matter is mostly carbon, and that is what makes soils able to support plant life. Organic matter retains water in the soil and makes nutrients more available and less volatile, all while minimizing erosion and nutrient loss. This organic "sponge" in the soil is capable of cushioning the pounding rain, dramatically increasing infiltration, retaining moisture for groundwater recharge, slowing runoff, holding life-supporting nutrients, and reducing surface temperature and evaporation.

Runoff from agriculture is now the largest water-quality problem in the United States. Regenerative soil management techniques such as winter cover crops can add about a half ton of carbon to each and every acre of soil. These techniques, along with forested streamside buffers, are needed to curb water pollution and sedimentation, and to sequester carbon.

Varying in thickness, topsoil is the only thing separating the air from unproductive subsoils, fractured bedrock, or other parent material that is not capable of sustaining much biological activity. During the Dust Bowl days, early soil conservationists often warned that the nearest desert was not hundreds of miles away, but just a few inches below our feet. These early conservationists knew that only good soil management could keep the desert away.

I counted the late Robert Rodale from Emmaus, Pennsylvania, as a friend and a tireless conservation hero. Rodale spent his life challenging the dominant agricultural view, which was largely insensitive to maintaining the life-giving natural vitality of organic soil. Rodale taught organic farming through his various magazines and understood that healthy topsoil is a relatively thin and fragile layer teeming with living matter. He taught us that healthy soil is a complex microhabitat for diverse forms of life, including bacteria, fungi, insects, earthworms, and an array of fresh and partially decomposed plant materials. With his many ongoing field experiments, Rodale demonstrated that from a chemical perspective, healthy soil may be difficult to analyze due to its diverse molecular composition, but from a biological perspective, it is easy to tell that it is not just sand, silt, and clay. Though Rodale is gone, Tim LaSalle, the current CEO of the Rodale Institute, has become an influential voice of reason promoting regenerative agriculture that has the potential, along with carbon-neutral energy, to pull atmospheric CO_2 back down to safe levels.

As I've noted in detail in this book, the amount of carbon in the atmosphere is at the point beyond which scientists say it can safely remain. In a recently published paper, James Hansen and others examined paleoclimate data that show that climate sensitivity is much greater than previously estimated.[2] They suggest that CO_2 will need to be reduced from its current 387 parts per million (ppm) to at most 350 ppm. They also warn that if the present overshoot of this CO_2 target is not brief, there is a possibility of "*seeding irreversible catastrophic effects on the planet*"(emphasis added).[3] Hansen and the others suggest a 350 ppm CO_2 target may be achievable by phasing out coal use except where CO_2 is captured and by adopting agricultural and forestry practices that sequester carbon.

Since emissions-control targets that take the planet's atmosphere up to 450 ppm or, worse, 550 ppm are no longer tenable in light of recent evidence, we must be aggressive not only in cutting total emissions from every significant source worldwide, but in finding ways to pull CO_2 from the air. We can also no longer ignore the increasing contributions of deforestation, poor forestry practices, climate-induced forest diseases, and forest fires. Nor can we pass up the opportunity to store carbon in agricultural soils all over the world through carefully monitored offsets in agricultural and forest carbon storage. Even so, since it would take decades, through methods such as aggressive soil and forest sequestration, to bring atmospheric carbon back to the 350 ppm range, we may still be in for a rough ride on an overheated planet.

The green revolution must now refocus on regenerative agriculture. Agricultural lands worldwide are going to be called upon to work harder to meet growing population demands for foods, forage, fiber, and biofuels. At the same time, soils will be under increasing climate-induced drought stress and carbon losses while confronted by intensive storms and massive flooding.

We must restore and rebuild the carbon content of soils worldwide. To build greater resilience in the twenty-first century, we must foster sound practices that regenerate healthy, sustainable soils. Rather than subsidizing commodities, agricultural policies must measure and reward carbon storage in the soils and other sustainable farming practices designed to protect air, water, and soil. Through better crop methods that operate both on a commercial scale and on a small scale, we can enhance carbon capture in soils to provide:

- Improved soil tilth (Organic matter loosens heavy clay and silty soils and stimulates recovery of the natural soil-building microorganisms in the soil.)
- Reduced sediment and nutrient runoff (Carbon is sticky and binds to nutrients, soil particles, and potential pollutants to keep them from escaping into the waterways.)
- Improved moisture-holding capacity and groundwater recharge

- Reduced dependency on fossil fuels for artificial fertilizers, such as ammonium nitrates, which have powerful heat-trapping off-gases
- Improved nutrient quality of food sources and reduced human exposure to harmful chemicals

Farming on any scale is a very difficult enterprise. Having worked on dairy farms and in orchards in my youth, I appreciate that farmers' lives consist of hard work, long hours, and small returns. Petrochemicals have been further squeezing farmers' returns. To avoid the high cost of inputs, sustainable farmers are striving for optimal yields and long-term profits, not maximum yields, high costs, and risky returns. These farmers have discovered biological alternatives to high-nitrogen fertilizers that produce both greater nitrogen fertility and dramatically increased carbon storage. They plan to increase their net returns as carbon offsets pay for carbon storage in agricultural soils. Regenerative agriculture practices are a benefit to farmers because they reduce energy, fertilizers, herbicides, and other production costs and increase long-term improvements in soil health. Good farming means greater nutrients in our food and less silt in streams, rivers, lakes, and estuaries by increasing water-holding capacity of the soil during droughts and floods. Good farming also creates a more durable and healthier soil ecosystem for native wildlife.

There is a link between impoverished lands, impoverished people, and climate change. The degraded condition of agricultural lands around the world, particularly on lands that have been farmed for millennia, should trouble us all, as it is part of the loss that has been accelerating all over the world during the past century. To make matters worse, there is no end in sight. We now have the capacity to destroy land faster than ever before in the history of civilization. We must learn the lessons from past generations and not allow our landscapes to become impoverished through agricultural practices that do not replenish organic matter and carbon in the soils. By working together to solve climate problems and degraded soils through regenerative agriculture, the world can once again have healthy soils and abundant farmlands. By restoring damaged lands with funding from carbon storage offsets and adaptation funds, even poor nations can revitalize and maintain food production and greater forest resources, and they can help avoid further degradation of important water supplies.

Can we reverse the trend in agricultural destruction and strive to restore the landscapes we have damaged? My answer is an emphatic yes. It is time to put the black back in degraded soils all over the world.

Many farmers already know how to restore soils by storing carbon; they just need help paying for the planting of hairy vetch and other soil-building winter cover crops. A farm-based organization called 25 x '25 is creating "a rallying cry" for renewable energy and carbon storage and is setting a goal for US farmers and forest landowners to get 25 percent of the nation's energy from renewable resources such as wind, solar, and biofuels by the year 2025 and to play a part in storing carbon in soils and trees. The group is committed to bringing new technologies to market and saving consumers money, reducing dependence on oil from the Middle East, and creating good new jobs in rural America, all the while helping to reduce urban smog and greenhouse gas emissions.

A number of years ago, while touring some farmland in York County, Pennsylvania, I met the county's "farmer of the year." He showed us his well-managed, productive farm and pointed out places where erosion ditches once crisscrossed fields when his dad owned the farm. He reflected on those days, saying, "My dad didn't leave much of a farm when he died." Listening to his story, I was reminded of a line in Proverbs that reads, "A good man leaves an inheritance to his children's children." This York County farmer impressed me as one who was practicing regenerative agriculture. He was farming not just to sustain production, but to heal damaged soils so he could pass on a good farm to his children.

Family farms that remain successful generation after generation are either on especially deep soils or the farmers have learned to care for their land by reducing the loss of top-soil and maintaining fertility and moisture-bearing capacity through rotational practices and enriching cover crops. In recent years, progressive farmers have increasingly adopted better minimum tillage methods, and they are fencing their streamsides with buffers to reduce stream bank erosion and nutrient runoff. Sustainable agriculture is marked by practices that emphasize cover crops, rotational grazing, crop diversity, and low or no inputs of chemical fertilizers and pesticides.

Farmers should not be measured just by the height of their corn or the number of bushels they grow per acre but by the color of their soil and the color of the water that runs off their land during storms. A good farmer is one who leaves productive soil for his children's children.

WHAT YOU CAN DO: GET YOUR HANDS DIRTY

Healthy black soils lead to healthier skies, so the more we can preserve healthy soils and regenerate lost or unhealthy soils, the better our planet's carbon cycle will function. Here are some suggestions to get you started on the path toward blacker, healthier soil:

1. Do as Michelle Obama is doing at the White House and grow your own organic vegetable garden—it's good for your kids' health, your wallet, and for the planet.
2. Compost and recycle all organic matter, including food and yard wastes, and create a thick, compost-covered, no-till garden. (I sold my rototiller thirty years ago and we have enjoyed productive, low-input, low-maintenance, no-till vegetable gardens ever since.)
3. Reduce the number of miles your food must travel by buying locally produced, organically grown foods when possible.
4. Support passage of legislation and a global agreement to cap carbon pollution, end deforestation, and generate a flow of carbon revenues from carbon pollution sources to landowners all over the world to help them store carbon in agricultural and forest lands.

CHAPTER 9

THE ROLE OF ENVIRONMENTAL EDUCATION

Global warming and a rapid deployment of solutions will touch and transform every facet of our modern world, including science, public policy, forestry, agriculture, business, and industry, and much more. I have attempted to highlight some of these challenges and solutions in earlier chapters, but there is also an important cultural dimension that must be addressed: Americans have lost touch with nature. This widespread disconnect may be a root cause of our current climate crisis.

Most Americans are living a life that is completely out of sync with nature. We are largely unaware of the climate threat because we live and travel in air-conditioned spaces. We spend our time staring at computer screens and television sets, and we are not aware of the many changes taking place in nature just outside our windows. One of the important steps we must take is to address the cultural piece of the puzzle. We need to consider and reevaluate our relationship and attitudes about nature, as they may be impairing our thinking about climate change.

Outdoors people, woodsmen, hikers, hunters, paddlers, birders, trappers, gardeners, and nature lovers do not need to be convinced by scientists that global warming is happening, because they have seen its early effects up close. Over the years, in my travels to all fifty states and beyond, I have encountered many interesting and knowledgeable outdoors people. You can see them coming, with their weather-worn faces, outdoor clothing, and leathery handshakes. After my climate presentations, they come up to tell their stories and share personal narratives about their special places and things they have seen change. With vivid detail, their stories invariably interweave time, place, and the forces of climate change into a powerful anecdote about how our world is changing. They know how global warming has affected and altered their landscapes and the hydrology of their rivers, and they see the myriad patterns of wildlife alterations that have happened over their lifetimes.

Outdoor people see what is happening to the natural world because they spend their lives outside. An elderly farmer from Russell, Kansas, reported seeing his first armadillo, on the road as it migrated north. A Quebec wildlife officer reported spotting his first opossum, lightly furred with a naked tail, exposed ears, and hairless feet. The species has been marching farther poleward year by year, from the southern United States into eastern Canada. A Montana fly angler shared a devastating story about Rogers Lake, which has been used for decades as a brood lake for reintroduction of the beautiful, troutlike, metallic purple Arctic grayling into Montana waters. During a prolonged drought and heat wave in Montana, when the lake's waters hit a record-setting 80°F, thousands of dead grayling, with their distinctive sail-like dorsal fins, floated to the surface.[1] A traditional Kentucky woman who earns extra money to support her family from trapping told me that excessively warm autumns are affecting the density, quality, and value of pelts.

Based on anecdotal examples from many outdoors people who know more about global warming than the general population, the National Wildlife Federation (NWF) decided to conduct a first-ever comprehensive nationwide survey of licensed hunters and anglers to understand their attitudes on global warming.[2] We commissioned Responsive Management of Harrisonburg, Virginia, to conduct the non-partisan survey because this firm had been polling for state fish and wildlife agencies for years and knew the sportsmen demographic space better than other polling firms.

From late March 2006 through April 2006, 1,031 hunters and anglers nationwide were polled, chosen randomly from state lists of individuals holding hunting and fishing licenses.[3] This poll revealed that a majority of sportsmen are witnessing the effects of global warming in their world. More than three-quarters of US hunters and anglers agreed that global warming is occurring, and the same percentage said they have observed changes in climate conditions where they live, such as warmer, shorter winters, hotter summers, earlier springs, less snow, and more.

We discovered from this poll that the majority of US sportsmen say global warming is an urgent problem that needs immediate action, and that they wanted clean energy solutions that create jobs and cut pollution from burning fossil fuels. We also discovered a deep reservoir of support, as the sportsmen said we have a moral responsibility to confront global warming with immediate actions necessary to address it. More than half said they believe the changes they see are related to global warming. Nearly three-quarters believe climate change either is currently affecting or will influence hunting or fishing conditions. On several occasions in recent years, NWF polled license-holding hunters and anglers all across the United States as representatives for those who spend time in the out-of-doors. We were surprised to find that half of those surveyed identified themselves as evangelical Christians. The number of sportsmen-evangelicals went to 65 percent in the South. Eighty-six percent agree that the federal government should provide incentives for industries to replace some energy from oil, gas, and coal with renewable energy sources such as wind and solar power. Eighty-four percent support federal incentives for companies that develop new energy-efficient technologies that reduce global warming, and 87 percent support federal incentives that make energy conservation technologies more affordable for all citizens.

In more recent NWF Action Fund polls, 80 percent of sportsmen polled believe the United States should be a world leader in addressing global warming. In each of these polls, respondents demonstrated a much higher recognition of the near-term threat of global warming on their local world than the public at large do, as measured by a number of other polls. For example, a January 2007 national survey by the Pew Research Center for the People and the Press found that only 55 percent (though still a majority) said global warming is a problem that requires immediate government action.[4] So being outdoors matters with respect to our attitudes and understandings about climate change and energy development.

Outdoors people understand the situation more clearly, and they want a new direction to protect what they have. They clearly support a major shift away from fossil fuels that produce global warming pollution and a shift toward developing a new generation of alternative and renewable energy sources. Overall, more than two-thirds (69 percent) of sportsmen said the nation is on the wrong track in meeting its energy needs. An overwhelming majority, 78 percent, say conserving more, developing fuel-efficient vehicles, and expanding the use of renewable sources are the best ways to address US energy needs, rather than drilling for more oil and gas within the United States.[5]

I have also been privileged to know and be mentored by a few people who spent their entire lives mostly outdoors, often on a single piece of land or in a rural region of the country. My father-in-law, Quincy Baird Hershey Sr., was one such person. Baird was trained as a taxidermist at the Carnegie Museum, and later served as state taxidermist with the Pennsylvania Museum while Gifford Pinchot was governor. He was a fur buyer and founder of the Hershey Fur Center, which later became Hershey International. Baird was one of the first sanctioned Boone and Crockett measurers and lived on the same land near Gettysburg, Pennsylvania, for ninety-two years.

As a boy, he and his grandfather drove a horse-drawn ice plow to score the ice to be cut on the nearby ponds. Every year at winter's peak, Baird and his family would gather together to cut the ice when it reached about eighteen inches thick. They stored the neatly cut ice blocks packed in sawdust in a nearby icehouse. Throughout the year, the Hershey family earned their living by delivering ice by wagon to the village of York Springs and to surrounding farms. In those days, families had zinc- or galvanized-lined ash, oak, and pine iceboxes with names like KleenKold, Norge, Porcelain, Defender, White Mountain Grand, Niagara Refrigeration, Wabash, North Pole, and Coolerator. In his last years, Baird noted that icebox companies were gone, and so was the thick ice of yesterday.

As the family tradition carried on for decades after the ice business disappeared, each year Baird measured the ice on the nearby pond at the peak of winter, taking careful notes in his daily journal. On his ninetieth birthday, he asked me to help him measure his ice. It was barely three inches thick. He warned, "I have not seen more than six inches of ice in the last twenty years. I do not need a scientist to tell me what is happening."

True outdoors people like Baird were much more common a generation or two ago. Living close to the land, intellectually open with an unquenchable childlike curiosity, they appreciated natural beauty and understood nature's relationships in ways that we simply cannot. Toward the end of his life, Baird had a heart attack. Expecting a near-death heart patient, I went to visit him in the cardiac care unit at the Hanover Hospital. Much to my surprise, I found Baird with several gardening books on roses and various papers sprawled over his movable bedside table. "What are you doing?" I asked. His response: "I didn't die yesterday, so I'm planning on making a new rose garden when I get out of here." Living close to nature and leaving a legacy was Baird's sustenance just as much as food, air, and water. I often think about his lifestyle and the stark contrast between one generation and their place-based lives and the current generation that moves on average every five years.[6] It seems we are always close to a computer screen in some big city and forever farther and farther away from nature and our homes. In a generation, we have lost vital links to the natural world and so much more.

Recently, I was on a flight from Washington, DC, to San Francisco. Sitting to the left of me in the window seat was a rather obese boy who was about ten years old. His mom put him on the plane to visit his dad in California. As soon as our plane was over ten thousand feet, the boy broke out his Game Boy and settled in for a long and intense session. After a couple of hours of this, our pilot came on the intercom and said, "Folks, off to our left is one of the best views you will ever see of the Grand Canyon." I watched the boy. His eyes never left the Game Boy, not even for a second. I was saddened that this child had no apparent interest in the wonders of nature below. Instead, he was mesmerized by a gadget. It occurred to me that I was witnessing firsthand an important American phenomenon that is having a profound impact on our children's future and the very future of nature itself.

Some might ask, "Why does it matter whether or not our kids go outside?" There is an important link between being outdoors, paying attention to the natural world and caring for nature, and having healthy bodies and minds. A recent study by Cornell researchers suggests that children who hike, fish, camp, or just spend time in the wild before age eleven are much more likely to grow up to be environmentally minded as adults. Their study indicates that participating in nature activities before age eleven is a "particularly potent pathway toward shaping both environmental attitudes and behaviors in adulthood."[7] According to the 2008 Outdoor Recreation Participation Report, more than 50 percent of Americans participated in outdoor recreation in 2007, getting outside 11.36 billion times—either close to home, in a nearby park, or on an overnight trip. At the same time, the report revealed an "11.6% decline in participation in outdoor activities among American children ages 6 to 17," with the sharpest declines among youth ages 6 to 12.[8]

American children are trending away from outdoor recreational pursuits, and environmental literacy has declined. American youth are now spending very little time out in nature, having largely abandoned the great outdoors for indoor pursuits. What is happening to our connection to nature, and where has our outdoor time gone? There are many signs that something major—something profoundly different—is happening to the basic connection between Americans and the outdoors. The signs are everywhere:

- A study published in *Early Childhood* in 2004 found that 70 percent of mothers reported that their children play outdoors less than they did as children.[9]
- In 2005, the Association for Childhood Education International reported that children's outdoor time is down by 40 percent over previous generations'.[10] Perhaps indoor people, spending much of their time in front of a television or computer, isolated in an air-conditioned space, can easily ignore global warming.
- In 2004, the Kaiser Family Foundation estimated that the average child now spends over six hours daily watching television, playing video games, or on a computer.[11]

That's a fourth of their day, a fourth of their life, and something we should all be concerned about, whether we're parents or not.

- Schools in Washington State with environmental education programs showed higher test scores on standardized tests in math, reading, writing, and listening.[12] Another recent study indicated that "among 8- to 9-year-old children, having 1 daily recess period of more than 15 minutes in length was associated with better teacher's rating of class behavior scores.[13]

It is too easy to just blame technology addictions for the change. There are other factors at play as well. Many suburban and urban parents perceive a lack of access to safe outdoor spaces. Others mention rising fuel prices with regard to outdoor vacations. Despite the trend, 93 percent of mothers report that they recognize the significant benefits of children spending more time outdoors for health and motor skill development reasons. Some 77 percent agreed that it improved childhood social skills, and 82 percent saw outdoor play as a way to improve a child's sense of self-worth.[14]

Years ago, kids burned plenty of calories playing outdoors. A study in *The Journal of Pediatrics*, "Physical Activity Recommendations for School-Age Youth," found that "our children are just not burning up those calories today."[15] The Centers for Disease Control and Prevention suggests that the missing ingredient for most kids is an hour per day of unstructured activity.[16] Researchers in such places as Chicago and Boston are studying how the nationwide childhood obesity epidemic may cause shorter life spans for the next generation. They conclude that, while we have enjoyed increases in expected life span for several decades, the new lack of childhood activity and its resulting extra pounds can lead to adult-onset diabetes and can actually shorten the average life span by three to five years.[17]

Comparing the boy on my flight with my own youth made me both proud and sad. As kids, we roamed for hours across the hills of northern Allegheny County, Pennsylvania, climbing trees, building forts in them and dams in the creeks. My mother would often remark that my brothers and I lived outdoors. I suspect you have spent a great deal of your childhood free time in outdoors too. I'm proud of our upbringing, our time spent outside in the dirt. But when I see kids such as this boy on the flight, I can't help but feel sad for him and what he's missing and ultimately will lack.

Spending so much time in screen space rather than green space is not something we should encourage. In fact, our moms were right. Being outside is healthier for a whole host of reasons. And the profound disconnect with nature is not limited to children. Adult outdoor behavior is changing as well. RoperASW reports that in 2001, a decades-long pattern of increasing outdoor recreation participation in the United States shifted dramatically downward. Ironically, the RoperASW report also documents convincingly that Americans of all ages see the importance of increased outdoor time. Of the twenty-seven outdoor activities the survey has been tracking for the American Recreation Coalition, twenty-one displayed a reduction while just six showed an increase. The National Park Service and many state parks departments report that attendance is down some 20 percent over the past ten years. Importantly, the RoperASW survey shows that the drop in participation is particularly noteworthy among young adults (19 percent to 24 percent less outdoor activity). This group of young people also reports high levels of access to the Internet.[18]

Out of the window of my home office where I write this, I look at several forested hilltops overlooking the Pine Creek Valley, where nine decades ago, Rachel Carson and her mother often roamed, looking for spring flowers. I cannot help but believe that those hours afield in western Pennsylvania had a profound influence on this great conservationist fostering a deep "sense of wonder." Carson must have surely remembered her hikes with her mom when she penned these words: "The years of early childhood are the time to prepare the soil. Once the emotions have been aroused—a sense of the beautiful; the excitement of the new and the unknown; a feeling of sympathy, pity, admiration, or love—then we wish for knowledge about the object of our emotional response. Once found, it has lasting meaning. It is more important to pave the way for the child to want to know than to put him on a diet of facts he is not ready to assimilate."[19]

While as a society we have largely disconnected from nature, we are still wholly dependent upon a healthy biosphere. In recent years, the interdependent relationship between humans and nature has been described through a wide-range of "ecosystem services" such as clean air, pure water, pharmaceuticals from nature, carbon storage in forests, soils, and tundra, and the many other benefits provided by nature for human benefit. Many years ago, at the time of the very first Earth Day, a noted French American microbiologist, René Dubos, warned, "Without the countless and immensely varied forms of life that the earth harbors, our planet would be just another fragment of the universe with a surface as drab as that of the moon and an atmosphere inhospitable to man. We human beings exist and enjoy life only by virtue of the conditions created and maintained on the surface of earth by the microbes, plants, and animals that have converted its inanimate matter into a highly integrated living structure."[20] In his landmark essay "The Conservation Ethic," Aldo Leopold warned that "civilization is not…the enslavement of a stable and constant earth. It is a state of mutual interdependent cooperation between human animals, other animals, plants, and the soil, which may be disrupted at any moment by the failure of any of them."[21] To Leopold's point, we must prevent the "failure of any of them" by developing an attitude of living in harmony with nature. Beyond the need to respect our physical interdependence with nature, Edward O. Wilson speaks of the spiritual dimension of nature in *The Diversity of Life*, saying that

> wilderness settles peace on the soul because it needs no help; it is beyond human contrivance. Wilderness is a metaphor of unlimited opportunity…We do not understand ourselves yet and descend farther from heaven's air if we forget how much the natural world means to us. Signals abound that the loss of life's diversity endangers not just the body but the spirit. If that much is true, the changes occurring now will visit harm on all generations to come.[22]

Kids of every age need to touch the earth and, as the Dixie Chicks suggest, "grow something wild and unruly."

They just need to be outside more for their own physical, emotional, and mental well-being. Gone are the days when the majority of kids spent hours at a time in the full flush of nature, in unstructured play exploring the hidden wonders under every rock and around every tree. Gone, too, are the days when kids slept under a blanket of stars.

What will become of wild places if our children, including the boy on the plane, know little of the mystery, the grace, the interconnectedness of all living things? We only save what we love, and we can love only what we know. Only by millions of people reconnecting with nature will nature have any chance for survival. We all need to reconnect with nature for the renewal of our minds and for the future of our planet. Otherwise, I fear our children will face an overheated world with little environmental knowledge or preparation to cope with the changes.

Time spent in untrammeled nature is vivid, multisensory, and memorable. We are touched in visceral ways with the power and immediacy of our surroundings. Through these full-throated experiences, our brains absorb enduring impulses coming all at once through our ears, eyes, fingers, and nose. Our memories are made that much more rich and durable by power of the simultaneous multiple stimuli around us. We literally absorb the place as it absorbs us.

As a child, I spent many hours afield with my father, who was a dog trainer and hunter. Dad died more than thirty years ago. Yet when I go to the woods of western Pennsylvania and smell a familiar plant or hear a distant crow on a crisp fall morning, my memories of being out in nature with Dad come flooding back in rich detail as if it were yesterday. In those moments, I can clearly hear his gravelly voice and I can see his ruddy face in the golden light of an early morning sun. I cherish those fleeting memories and the connections that they restore.

I would urge every parent, grandparent, aunt, or uncle to make memories in nature with the children in your life. They will scarcely remember watching television with you, but in their heart, they will hold on to the times they spent in the wild with you. Equally important, you can help awaken their ecological understandings and forge a love for nature that will serve them for a lifetime.[23]

WHAT YOU CAN DO: INVOLVE YOURSELF AND YOUR FAMILY

Children are greatly affected by the attitudes and actions of their parents and role models. Get outside, and take them with you. You'll all benefit from the exercise, the air, and the unavoidable connection to nature and wildlife.

1. Teach your children how to take care of soil in your yard and garden. Involve them in the planning and planting process, as well as in the maintenance of those areas and soils.

2. Take your children or grandchildren on trips to national parks and different types of ecosystems to help expand their experience of nature and wildlife.

3. If you can't travel, help your children explore and enjoy the natural world through NWF's children's magazines: *Ranger Rick*, *Your Big Backyard*, and *Wild Animal Baby*.

4. Give your kids unstructured outdoor play time—it makes them happier, healthier, and even smarter. To learn more about NWF's Be Out There initiative, visit www.nwf.org/beoutthere.

5. Invite your friends, family, and neighbors together for a kitchen table study of global warming and its effects on nature, both local and national, and what you as individuals and a group could do about them. You can do many things to make a difference if you allow your imaginations to flow.

CHAPTER 10

LAST CHANCE

...and for destroying those who destroy the earth.
—Revelation 11:18

Some years ago, I was traveling with friend and colleague
Charlie Shaw. We were on our way to a meeting with several
volunteers when with no warning, Charlie pulled the car onto
the shoulder, leapt out, and ran behind the car and down the
berm of Interstate 95. I watched with amazement as Charlie
waited for a break in traffic. Then he darted across the highway to a small turtle creeping along the roadside. Charlie
and the turtle studied each other as huge eighteen-wheelers
zoomed by just feet away. The turtle apparently grew bored
and moved on. Once Charlie figured out where the turtle
wanted to go—which happened to be across the highway—
Charlie picked him up, waited for a break in traffic, zipped
across, and put the turtle well up the grassy embankment on
the far side. Then he jogged back to the car, got in, and we
drove off. "An endangered species?" I queried teasingly. "Just
a box turtle," Charlie responded. "I hate to see those little
guys get hit."

Charlie grew up in western North Carolina at a time when farmers would pick up box turtles they came across while plowing. Often, a farmer would stop his tractor and secure a turtle on top of a fence post with baling twine to keep it safe from the plows. A pleasant chore for the children at the end of the day was to walk the fence lines to release the turtles perched on the posts, their legs waving in the air. Children enjoyed watching the turtles disappear to safety across the contrasting ribbons of freshly plowed fields in a setting sun.

Charlie died unexpectedly on his way to a National Wildlife Federation (NWF) convention in Denver. I shared that story at his memorial in Denver, not to focus on what he did, but to remind his friends from across the country who Charlie was. For years after that, people who heard that story would tell me about turtles they rescued. People like Charlie still believe turtles are worth saving. They make small, unseen, and unapplauded gestures just because it's the right thing to do for the future of nature. For them, it's easy to help a turtle cross a road, or toss papers into a recycling bin, or replace energy-guzzling conventional light bulbs with LED or florescent bulbs.

Thank goodness for caring people who are willing to take the small steps that add up to real declines in energy use. Yet, as good as these individual actions may be, collectively they are not enough to protect the planet. Even the recent stimulus package and a number of state- and city-based climate and clean energy initiatives have not been big enough to jump-start the clean energy economy.

Americans deserve better energy choices that eliminate our dependence on fossil fuels with volatile prices set by the oil cartel. A cap on carbon pollution will drive investments in clean, reliable, made-in-America energy technology such as wind, solar, and geothermal. We can create a strong economic recovery with millions of new domestic jobs in the natural resources, clean energy, and energy efficiency sectors, all the while reducing global warming pollution and protecting the nature of tomorrow. We must transform our entire energy economy to end carbon emissions while creating durable US jobs. This action has the added benefit of keeping energy dollars and soldiers at home.

We are conducting a massive planetary experiment outside the range of human experience or competence. If new coal-fired power plants continue to be deployed at a rate of one every three or four days, we will surely double airborne CO_2 in as little as thirty-five years. We must call on China and India and the developing world to abandon investments in twentieth-century technologies, and we all must end profligate consumption of fossil fuels while there is still hope. We need to do everything possible to end CO_2 emissions while at the same time minimizing further global warming by sequestering carbon in agricultural soils and in forests.

In their study published in January 2009 in the *Proceedings of the National Academy of Sciences*, Susan Solomon and her coauthors suggest that while some of the greenhouse gases that contribute to climate change such as methane and nitrous oxide will abate within a few years after they are controlled, this is not the case for the most ubiquitous pollutant, CO_2.[1] In a National Public Radio interview, Solomon warned, "People have imagined that if we stopped emitting carbon dioxide that the climate would go back to normal in 100 years or 200 years. What we're showing here is that's not right. It's essentially an irreversible change that will last for more than a thousand years."[2]

We cannot unfry an egg. Nor can we simply pull CO_2 from the skies once it has been dispersed. We are at a critical moment in human history. It is now clear: if pollution is left unchecked, we are on the pathway to destructive and irreversible temperature increases. If we act now, we can reduce the damage. We must accept what we cannot change, and we must find the courage to change what our children simply cannot accept. If we fail to grasp that relatively small daily changes in the planet's average temperature will precipitate future dramatic consequences, we will miss the opportunity to speak when words still matter. We must not fail to act while our actions still count.

During a recent flight, my plane was delayed by mechanical problems. After a frustrating forty-five-minute wait on the ground wondering if I would make my connecting flight, the pilot came on the intercom and put things in perspective. "I'd rather be down here wishing I was up there than up there wishing we were down here." Similarly, we need to keep CO_2 levels down here so that our children will not be up there wishing they could somehow get back down here.

As the atmospheric, terrestrial, and marine systems continue to degrade at an alarming pace, for the sake of all children of all time, I beg you to join together to avoid a climate crisis. If we don't tackle climate change soon, it will tackle us. It is that simple. It may be hard for some to believe that you and I can make a meaningful difference, but I'm here to tell you that individual action is the only thing that works for real change in a democracy.

As a teenager, I had the good fortune to be mentored by Ralph Abele, a scout leader and World War II hero who believed in the power of the individual and the inherent virtue of stubbornness. Ralph was also a courageous and tireless leader in the conservation movement who in his final editorial with the Pennsylvania Fish Commission wrote, "The unique power bestowed on each individual human being to do good and even change the course of history is quite often underestimated…One person with enough tenacity can dig in his heels and say, 'This much and no more.'" Ralph often reminded his young followers to "beware of the cause that you choose for this kind of stubbornness because you will surely prevail! There are great causes to be followed, and victory always starts with one person hanging on by his teeth and saying, 'I will never give in'…I insist that if one is stubborn enough—immovable, unchangeable, inexorable—he can and will prevail."[3] While I wish Ralph were still alive to lead the fight in this great battle, I now must be thankful that others with courage and tenacity stand in his place.

Moral Authority

With an earthworm dangling from its beak, a robin was limping along the trail a few feet in front of me. Feigning an inability to fly by drooping a wing, the robin was drawing me away from her featherless nestlings in a nearby tree. Risking her very life for them, this robin reminded me of our innate duty to sacrifice and even to risk ourselves if called upon to protect our offspring and other innocents. For the sake of the next generation, the innocents, and for the wildlife of tomorrow, we must act now.

Rachel Carson warned, "The History of Life on earth has been a history of interaction between living things and their surroundings. To a large extent, the physical form and the habits of the earth's vegetation and its animal life have been molded by the environment. Considering the whole span of earthly time, the opposite effect, in which life actually modifies its surroundings, has been relatively slight. Only within the moment of time represented by the present century has one species—man—acquired significant power to alter the nature of his world."[4]

Carson was right. Humankind is vitally linked into the web of life. Unlike other species, we have enormous power to change it, and we are altering the nature of the world in profound ways. Along with fellow travelers in nature, we humans cannot make it to the future without functioning ecosystems—including healthy, productive oceans, forests, waters, and soils. To think otherwise is an outrageous, prideful disregard of the laws of nature, and pure hubris.

IT IS TIME TO WORK TOGETHER

We must end carbon pollution now. While environmental challenges facing the world are obviously complex and arduous, solving global warming is not so much a technical problem as it is a political one. We need to work across political lines to solve the climate crisis.

Congress needs to pass a science-based energy plan, and the administration must keep the pressure on Congress to get this done so it can carry a sound plan to Copenhagen in December 2009 and lead the world in passing a global treaty requiring every nation to do its part to stop global warming.

Congress must rewrite our national energy laws to reflect current realities in order to end pollution and build a clean, domestically supplied energy economy. To do that, lawmakers on both sides must put aside strongly held ideological barriers.

Throughout the history of the nation's conservation and environmental movements, from President Theodore Roosevelt to Senator John Heinz (a Republican senator from Pennsylvania who partnered with Senator Tim Wirth, a Democrat from Colorado, to curb acid rain), there have been courageous leaders who have stepped across the aisle to do what was right for the planet. Only eight Republican House members understood their moral duty to work in a bipartisan way to protect nature and stop pollution by voting for the American Clean Energy and Security Act in June 2009.[5]

The spirit of bipartisanship has been crushed in recent decades as the few remaining moderate Republican members of Congress have become fearful that they will become targets of Rush Limbaugh and his ilk. They are running scared. They know that the Club for Growth, the well-funded voice of laissez-faire capitalism, and other far-right groups have defeated responsible conservation-minded Republican lawmakers, such as Congressman Wayne Gilchrest (MD), in primary elections. The recent trend away from stewardship started in the early 1990s when Republicans developed a theme called the "Contract with America" that won elections for them. Their simple message: "Government is the problem, not the solution." They promised to roll back wetlands protections and other environmental protection laws, defund enforcement efforts, and block other consumer protection programs in finance, food, and drug safety. Well, it worked!

Blind ideology is the greatest challenge to a new energy future. Many Republicans are unwilling or unable to acknowledge the large body of climate science and address the dangers of global warming. Others openly promote climate pseudoscience as justification for inaction. Because we tend to listen to and trust our party's leaders, polls have shown a gap between the number of Republicans and Democrats who believe global warming is an urgent threat. While a majority of Republican voters support action, they trail Democrats in their understanding of the urgency of the threat.[6]

In his book *The Structure of Scientific Revolutions*, author Thomas Samuel Kuhn examines why obvious scientific evidence is sometimes obscure. He coined the phrase *paradigm blindness* to explain that it is not possible to understand or even see a new paradigm through a flawed conceptual framework and the terminology of a rival paradigm.[7] Perhaps the growing partisan divide and paradigm blindness over environmental protection reflects a tendency to put misplaced faith in party leaders, ideological pundits, and news shows that reflect polarizing ideology over science. If some members of Congress believe global warming is a liberal hoax, they cannot see the scientific evidence, no matter how extensive it may be. In the face of Arctic ice shrinking by 40 percent or forest fires increasing by a factor of four, if global warming is denied, paradigm blindness has set in, preventing those affected from seeing the truth.

Both parties must reject ideology-based, uninformed opinions heard on talk radio and ignore the anti-intellectual, antiscience political dinosaurs on Washington's K Street. Instead, lawmakers must look to mainstream scientific communities from all over the world whose members have published vast volumes of scientific evidence in peer-reviewed journals. We must also quit depending on yesterday's energy companies to give us tomorrow's energy solutions, and we must reject their false and misleading messages broadcast in unrelenting television advertisements. No lawmaker should be allowed to give a weak response or work with well-funded oil, utility, and coal foes to thwart climate legislation.

Looking ahead, I cling to the hope that all Americans will cut through the cynical obfuscation that has caused paradigm blindness in the halls of Congress and help lawmakers discover the truth about what lies ahead for all humanity. Voter pressure is the only thing that can overcome such blindness.

We must work with a new spirit of cooperation, encouraging and supporting one another and constantly pressing forward. I appeal especially to conservative Republican voters who have repeatedly been told that global warming is a political conspiracy. Search your hearts and join with the rest of America to care for all creation. This is not about being liberal or conservative. Global warming will harm children on the right as well as those on the left. This is about doing the right thing.

We need to be a cohesive nation to win this one. This is our opportunity to sacrifice, not in war but in an all-out battle to end pollution and protect nature. We can still make a difference for the next generations if we are willing to mobilize in an effort to change our sources of energy.

Let's look afresh at our nation's energy policies, which incentivize fossil fuel exploitation. They were enacted for a different time and purpose, long ago. A bold new legal framework is needed to help clean-energy entrepreneurs in emerging enterprises deliver carbon-free energy over an efficient, smart high-voltage national energy grid. We must establish enforceable energy goals for commercial and residential buildings and broad standards to unleash architects and engineers to design and build carbon-neutral and carbon-negative buildings. We must also envision new strategies for carbon-free transportation systems using battery-powered cars, high-speed rail, and innovative urban transportation strategies that use wind, solar, and carbon-negative biogas sources. Unless we all act to demand new laws to stop CO_2 pollution and help soils and forests reclaim CO_2 from the sky, the world will be in deep trouble.

Everyone around the world must be involved. We must warn others in developing nations of the destructive ecological forces that will be triggered by a rapidly changing climate. With long-term commitments to a shared outcome, the viability of planet earth, people all over can act with their hands and feet, while others can give support with their wallets or purses. In unity, not necessarily in uniformity, we must plan thoughtfully, marshal the facts, stay informed, and work with professionals and with others of every political stripe to solve this planetary threat.

The good news is that Americans are coming together as never before to reinvent this nation's energy future. Outdoors people, new energy leaders, farmers, foresters, college and high school students, people of faith, and millions of other voices for environmental justice are standing together for change. I am especially pleased that in 2008 a quarter of a million college students pledged to work together to solve this crisis, and they voted for change in record numbers.

They are following up by demanding action from the new Congress. Twelve thousand students showed up for an inspiring PowerShift Rally in Washington, DC, and to lobby Congress, in early March 2009. This awakening will realign politics in the United States to tackle the climate crisis.

In a speech to NWF members in Pittsburgh on May 1, 2009, speaking about a bipartisan "America's Path to Progress" initiative aimed at solving the climate crisis, Roberta Combs, the president of the Christian Coalition of America, pointed out that "as individuals we can make a difference; working together as a team we can make a miracle."[8]

WE ALONE HOLD THE KEYS TO THEIR FUTURE

Global warming is poised to do irreparable harm to the children of the world, taking away the opportunities that we have known. Unattended, it will foreclose hope for a sustainable planet. It will trigger uncountable extinctions and disrupt critically important ecosystems through droughts, floods, and fires. It will inundate coastal cities, compromise agricultural productivity, and interfere with life-supporting ecosystem services, leaving a wide swath of human suffering in its wake. Unless we confront the dangers now, we will unintentionally cause enormous damage to both the natural world and the built environment. We will threaten the very future of our children.

Will the United States, consumed by massive debt, a faltering economy, lingering wars, political divisions, and other worries in life, capitulate to this juggernaut? Let us not just drift aimlessly into an unprecedented climate catastrophe. We all must pull back from our addictive, overcommitted pace of daily living to recognize what Charles Hummel called our greatest danger, becoming slaves to the "tyranny of the urgent," letting those things that seem so pressing at the moment crowd out those things that are truly most important in the long haul.[9] In a moment of mental distraction or lapse in judgment, our lives can be devastated beyond words by the unintended consequences of our actions.

Far too often I have read heartbreaking accounts of a good, hardworking, loving parent who, half-awake or in a distracted moment on their way to work, forgot to drop their toddler at the daycare center. One such parent left Cameron, a sleeping three-year-old boy, helplessly strapped into a safety seat. Somehow, Cameron woke up, wiggled free from his seat, retrieved a spare key, and died trying to turn the ignition so he could open a window and avoid the overpowering greenhouse effect of sunlight pouring through auto glass. Will we, lost in our distractions, disbelief, and denials, ignore the unintended consequences of bad energy choices upon our children and their world? We cannot leave our children to fend on their own in an overheated world. We alone hold the keys to their future.

We have this final opportunity to put our children first. Unborn children do not have a say in the matter if you and I do not give them voice. We must find the stubborn courage to pressure our elected leaders. Most of all, we need to begin living sacrificially while focusing on change. Matters of moral importance like climate change call each of us to do what is right with humility, duty, and obligation, regardless of personal hardships, in order to protect the ecological integrity of the earth for future generations.

During America's greatest hours, we were united as one people. At the beginning of World War II, my father signed up for the US Army Air Force in an enlistment campaign called "Goodbye, my dear, I'll be back in a year." He returned home not a year later, but at the end of the war. Never once did he complain about the extra years that he served his country. I am thankful for past generations who stood for freedom and justice and defended others with their blood. How can we to do anything less for those who come after us?

Let us rise up as Americans, working together to create a safe energy economy and to give voice to this great healing opportunity while there is still time. For the sake of all children, please join with me in this effort to avoid a climate crisis and keep wildlife thriving. I have a note taped to my computer monitor with these simple words: "Keep your destination in view." Daily, it reminds me that climate stabilization must be our common destination. We must keep our eyes on that prize. Please join me in this fight. Together, we can be "stubborn, immovable, unchangeable, inexorable," and we will prevail!

WHAT YOU CAN DO: FIGHT FOR VALUABLE ECOSYSTEMS

One of my favorite places as a child, Lake Erie, has been damaged by numerous conventional threats and as a result is much more vulnerable to climate change. To provide some needed protection and resilience to this important ecosystem and to those near you, we must remove or reduce as many threats as possible and practical, and that will cost money. Climate security legislation should generate revenues from the auction of carbon credits, some of which must be devoted to adequately fund needed adaptation measures to protect important and endangered ecosystems like the Great Lakes, the Chesapeake Bay, coastal Louisiana, the Everglades, and Puget Sound, as well as the people who depend on them.

We must be a voice for wildlife and for our children. It is time to ask you to take an important first or perhaps next step as a volunteer. By advocating for new climate and economic security laws, policies, and international treaties, together we can push our elected officials to lead. You and I must urge every senator and House member, regardless of party affiliation, to stand up for a new energy path that is clean, renewable, and affordable. Let's reject incrementalism, as we no longer have time for it. We cannot go slowly. In this precious little time we have to solve the planetary crisis, let us work together.

Besides those political and public steps suggested in the sidebar in chapter 7, the most important thing we can do at this time is ask Congress to enact a Federal Climate Security Law to cap carbon emissions, to provide sufficient funding from carbon revenues for consumers to implement energy efficiencies, for research and development of new technologies, and to fund ecosystem adaptation and restoration. In January 2008, a group of six hundred wildlife scientists (including most of the top names in the field) sent a letter to Congress urging passage of legislation to reduce greenhouse gases consistent with science and to include substantial funding for wildlife and ecosystem restoration from carbon fees. Add your voice to this effort in any and every way possible. It may prove to be the most important legislation of our time.

NOTES

PREFACE

1. Chris D. Thomas, Alison Cameron, Rhys E. Green, Michael Bakkenes, Linda J. Beaumont, Yvonne C. Collingham, Barend F. N. Erasmus, et al., "Extinction Risk from Climate Change," *Nature* 427 (January 8, 2004): 145–148.

2. A. Fischlin, G. F. Midgley, J. T. Price, R. Leemans, B. Gopal, C. Turley, M. D. A. Rounsevell, et al., "Ecosystems, Their Properties, Goods, and Services," in *Climate Change 2007: Impacts, Adaptation and Vulnerability*, ed. M. L. Parry, O. F. Canziani, J. P. Palutikof, P. J. van der Linden, and C. E. Hanson (Cambridge, MA: Cambridge Univ. Press, 2007), 211–272.

INTRODUCTION: THE NATURE OF TOMORROW

Epigraph. John Tyndall, *Fragments of Science: A Series of Detached Essays, Addresses, and Reviews Complete in One Volume* (New York: A. L. Burt, 1890), 394.

1. J. T. Overpeck, M. Sturm, J. A. Francis, D. K. Perovich, M. C. Serreze, R. Benner, E. C. Carmack, et al., *Arctic System on Trajectory to New, Seasonally Ice-Free State. EOS, Transactions, American Geophysical Union* 86, no. 34 (August 2005): 309.

2. Paul Sisco, "NASA Scientists See Hastened Arctic Warming," *Voice of America*, January 9, 2008, www.voanews.com/english/archive/2008 -01/2008-01-09-voa12.cfm?CFID=75590361&CFTOKEN=65399926.

3. Al Gore, "The Climate Project: Training for Faith Leaders" (Nashville, Tennessee, October 8, 2008).

4. National Wildlife Federation, *National Opinion Survey of Hunters and Anglers* (Harrisonburg, VA: Responsive Management, March/April 2006), www.targetglobalwarming.org/files/Toplines_National _FINAL.pdf.

5. A. Fischlin, G. F. Midgley, J. T. Price, R. Leemans, B. Gopal, C. Turley, M. D. A. Rounsevell, et al., "Ecosystems, Their Properties, Goods, and Services," in *Climate Change 2007: Impacts, Adaptation and Vulnerability*, ed. M. L. Parry, O. F. Canziani, J. P. Palutikof, P. J. van der Linden, and C. E. Hanson (Cambridge, MA: Cambridge Univ. Press, 2007), 211–272.

6. Steven B. Oates, *A Woman of Valor: Clara Barton and the Civil War* (New York: Free Press, 1995), 78.

7. Rachel Carson, "Global Thermostat," in *The Sea Around Us* (New York: Oxford Univ. Press, 1951), 169–188.

8. Rachel Carson, *The Edge of the Sea* (Boston: Houghton Mifflin, 1955), 28.

9. John Brashear, *John Brashear: An Autobiography* (Cambridge, MA: Riverside Press, 1924), 235. (This quote comes from a lecture entitled "Science of the Beautiful in Commonplace Things," given at the annual meeting of the Society of Mechanical Engineers, New York, 1918).

10. Naomi Oreskes, "Beyond the Ivory Tower: The Scientific Consensus on Climate Change," *Science* 306, no. 5702 (December 2004): 1686.

11. Proverbs 13:22 (New International Version).

PART I: THE SCIENCE AND THE RAPIDLY APPROACHING REALITY

CHAPTER 1: CLOSER THAN YOU THINK

Epigraph. Svante Arrhenius, 1896. "On the influence of carbonic acid in the air upon the temperature of the ground," *Philosophical Magazine and Journal of Science* 41, no. 5: 237–276.

1. Oliver Trager, ed., "Our Poisoned Planet: Can We Save It?" (New York: Facts on File, 1989), 116.

2. Wallace S. Broecker, "Before the US Senate Committee on Environment and Public Works: Subcommittee on Environmental Protection and Subcommittee on Hazardous Wastes and Toxic Substances," *Daily Digest*, Wednesday, January 28, 1987; D92 (Bound vol. D32-D35), www.lib.ncsu.edu/congbibs/senate/100dgst1.html.

3. Wallace S. Broecker spent his impressive fifty-two-year career at Columbia University specializing in radioisotope dating and in the

fields of oceanography and paleoclimatology. In 1985, he warned of the possibility of abrupt climate change, suggesting that the conveyorlike circulation in the Atlantic Ocean constituted the climate system's Achilles' heel.

4. Lenny Bernstein, Peter Bosch, Osvaldo Canziani, Zhenlin Chen, Renate Christ, Ogunlade Davidson, William Hare, et al., *Climate Change 2007 Synthesis Report for Policymakers* (report from the IPCC Plenary XXVII conference, Valencia, Spain, November 12–17, 2007), 5, www.ipcc.ch/pdf/assessment-report/ar4/syr/ar4_syr_spm.pdf.

5. Climate changes are at work in the United States and are projected to grow. Thomas R. Karl, Jerry M. Melillo, and Thomas C. Peterson, eds., *Global Climate Change Impacts in the United States* (New York: Cambridge Univ. Press, 2009), www.globalchange.gov/usimpacts.

6. Scripps Institute of Oceanography, "Charles David Keeling: Climate Science Pioneer: 1928–2005," University of California–San Diego, http://sio.ucsd.edu/keeling.

7. Trager, ed., "Our Poisoned Planet," 114. (Charles L. Hosler is now professor emeritus of meteorology, senior vice president for research, and dean emeritus of the graduate school at Penn State University.)

8. Jeff Barnard, "Researchers Track Dust, Soot from China," Boston. com News, July 13, 2007, www.boston.com/news/education/higher/articles/2007/07/13/researchers_track_dust_soot_from_china.

9. Rob Gutro, "NASA Study Finds Soot May Be Changing the Arctic Environment," *Earth Observatory*, March 23, 2005, http://earthobservatory.nasa.gov/Newsroom/view.php?old=2005032318608.

10. Pat Brennan, "Research Tracks Arctic Warming's Correlation to 'Dirty Snow,'" *The Orange County Register*, January 16, 2008.

11. NASA, "Keeling Curve," image of the day, Earth Observatory, September 22, 2008, http://earthobservatory.nasa.gov/IOTD/view.php?id=5620.

12. J. T. Houghton, L. G. Meira Filho, B. A. Callander, N. Harris, A. Kattenberg, and K. Maskell, *Climate Change 1995: The Science of Climate Change* (Cambridge, MA: Cambridge Univ. Press, 1996), 572.

13. Bernstein et al., *Climate Change 2007 Synthesis Report*.

14. Associated Press, "NASA Warming Scientist: 'This Is the Last Chance,'" *USA Today*, June 24, 2008.

15. This tachometer metaphor was originally used by Bill McKibben. Bill McKibben, "Civilization's Last Chance," *Los Angeles Times*, May 11, 2008.

16. J. Hansen, L. Nazarenko, R. Ruedy, Mki. Sato, J. Willis, A. Del Genio, D. Koch, et al., "2005: Earth's Energy Imbalance: Confirmation and Implications," *Science* 308, no. 5727: 1431–1435.

17. J. Hansen, M. Sato, P. Kharecha, D. Beerling, R. Berner, V. Masson-Delmotte, M. Pagani, et al., "Target Atmospheric CO_2: Where Should Humanity Aim?" Submitted April 7, 2008 (v1), last revised October 15, 2008 (this version, v3), *Open Atmos. Sci. J.* 2 (2008): 217–231.

18. M. Rigby et al., "Renewed Growth of Atmospheric Methane," *Geophysical Research Letters* 35 (2008): L22805.

19. D. A. Rothrock, Y. Yu, and G. A. Maykut, "Thinning of the Arctic Sea-Ice Cover," *Geophysical Research Letters* 26 (1999): 3469–3472.

20. National Research Council, *Understanding Climate Change Feedbacks* (Washington, DC: National Academies Press, 2003).

21. Seth Borenstein, "Ominous Arctic Melt Worries Experts," Associated Press, December 12, 2007.

22. Wieslaw Maslowski, presentation at the American Geophysical Union meeting in San Francisco, December 12, 2007, as reported by Jonathan Amos in "Arctic Summers Ice-free 'by 2013,'" BBC News, San Francisco, http://news.bbc.co.uk/2/hi/science/nature/7139797.stm.

23. National Snow and Ice Data Center, "Arctic Sea Ice Still on Track for Extreme Melt," *Arctic Sea Ice News & Analysis*, June 3, 2008, www.nsidc.org/arcticseaicenews/2008/060308.html.

24. National Snow and Ice Data Center, "Arctic Sea Ice Reaches Lowest Extent for 2008," press release, September 16, 2008.

25. M. C. Serreze, A. P. Barrett, J. C. Stroeve, D. N. Kindig, and M. M. Holland, "The Emergence of Surface-based Arctic Amplification," *The Cryosphere* 3 (2009): 11–19.

26. Robert W. Corell, "Focus on Climate Change: The Arctic Bellwether," *Foreign Service Journal* (February 2008): 28.

27. Robert W. Corell, "Arctic Climate Impact Assessment" (testimony before the US Senate Committee on Commerce, Science and Transportation, March 3, 2004), http://groundtruthinvestigations.com/documents/climatechange.html.

28. Rajendra, K. Pachauri, opening remarks, opening ceremony of the UNFCCC COP 14, Poznán, Poland, December 1, 2008, www.ipcc.ch/graphics/speeches/rajendra-pachauri-poznan-01-december-08.pdf.

29. G. M. Woodwell, F. T. MacKenzie, R. A. Houghton, M. Apps, E. Gorham, and E. Davidson, "Biotic Feedbacks in the Warming of the Earth," *Climatic Change* 40 (1998): 495–518.

30. Seth Borenstein, "Scientists Find New Global Warming Time-Bomb," Associated Press, September 7, 2006.

31. K. M. Walter, S. A. Zimov, J. P. Chanton, D. Verbyla, and F. S. Chapin III, "Methane Bubbling from Siberian Thaw Lakes as a Positive Feedback to Climate Warming," *Nature* 443 (2006): 71–75.

32. "Bad Sign for Global Warming: Thawing Permafrost Holds Vast Carbon Pool," Earth & Climate, *e! Science News*, September 3, 2008, http://esciencenews.com/articles/2008/09/03/bad.sign.global.warming.thawing.permafrost.holds.vast.carbon.pool.

33. Susan Q. Stranahan, "Melting Arctic Ocean Raises Threat of 'Methane Time Bomb,'" *Yale Environment 360*, October 30, 2008, http://e360.yale.edu/content/feature.msp?id=2081.

34. Bruce A. Buffett, "Clathrate Hydrates," *Annual Review of Earth and Planetary Sciences* 28 (May 2000): 477–507.

35. N. Shakhova, I. Semiletov, A. Salyuk, D. Kosmach, and N. Bel'cheva, "Methane Release on the Arctic East Siberian Shelf," *Geophysical Research Abstracts* 9, no. 01071 (2007).

36. Steve Connor, "The Methane Time Bomb," *The Independent* (London), September 23, 2008.

37. Ibid.

38. Volker Mrasek, "Melting Methane—A Storehouse of Greenhouse Gases Is Opening in Siberia," *Spiegel International*, April 17, 2008, www.spiegel.de/international/world/0,1518,547976,00.html.

39. Martin Kennedy, David Mrofkal, and Chris von der Borch, "Snowball Earth Termination by Destabilization of Equatorial Permafrost Methane Clathrate," *Nature* 453 (May 29, 2008): 642–645.

40. Martin Kennedy, "Large Release of Methane Could Cause Abrupt and Catastrophic Climate Change as Happened 635 Million Years Ago, UCR-led Study Warns," news release, Univ. of California–Riverside, May 28, 2008, http://newsroom.ucr.edu/cgi-bin/display.cgi?id=1849.

41. Biomes are regional ecosystems with distinctive biological communities that are well adapted to historic climatic conditions, soils, and other ecological factors.

42. Nancy Macdonald, "Climate Change and Forests: Canadian Forest Service's Approach," *AFC Media Corner*, April 21, 2005, http://cfs.nrcan.gc.ca/news/32.

43. *Terra Daily*, "Beetles May Doom Canada's Carbon Reduction Target," Flora and Fauna, April 23, 2008, www.terradaily.com/reports/Beetles_may_doom_Canadas_carbon_reduction_target_study_999.html.

44. A. L. Westerling, H. G. Hidalgo, D. R. Cayan, and T. W. Swetnam, "Warming and Earlier Spring Increase Western U.S. Forest Wildfire Activity," *Science* 313, no. 5789 (August 18, 2006): 940–943.

45. Melanie Lenart, "Scientists Seek Fire-Frequency Timeline, Global Climate Connections in Tree Rings, Charcoal," *UA News*, April 17, 2002, http://uanews.org/node/6292.

46. James Heath, Edward Ayres, Malcolm Possell, Richard D. Bardgett, Helaina I. J. Black, Helen Grant, Phil Ineson, et al., "Rising Atmospheric CO_2 Reduces Sequestration of Root-Derived Soil Carbon," *Science* 309, no. 5741 (September 9, 2005): 1711–1713.

47. Tim Radford, "Huge Rise in Siberian Forest Fires Puts Planet at Risk, Scientists Warn Krasnoyarsk," *The Guardian* (London), May 31, 2005.

48. "Death Toll in Australian Wildfires Above 150," Buzzle.com, February 9, 2009, www.buzzle.com/articles/death-toll-in-australian-wildfires -above-150.html.

49. Australian Bureau of Meteorology, *Special Climate Statement 17: The Exceptional January-February 2009 Heatwave in Southeastern Australia* (report, National Climate Centre, February 9, 2009), www .bom.gov.au/climate/current/statements/scs17c.pdf.

50. P. J. van Mantgem, N. L. Stephenson, J. C. Byrne, L. D. Daniels, J. F. Franklin, P. Z. Fulé, M. E. Harmon, et al., "Widespread Increase of Tree Mortality Rates in the Western United States," *Science* 323 (2009): 521–524.

51. Catherine Brahic, "Tree Deaths Double across Western US," *NewScientist*, January 22, 2009, www.newscientist.com/article/ dn16469-tree-deaths-double-across-western-us.html.

52. Y. Malhi, J. T. Roberts, R. A. Betts, T. J. Killeen, W. Li, and Carlos A. Nobre, "Climate Change, Deforestation, and the Fate of the Amazon," *Science* 319, no. 5860 (January 11, 2008): 169–172; and Y. Malhi, L. E. O. C. Aragão, D. Galbraith, C. Huntingford, R. Fisher, P. Zelazowski, S. Sitch, et al., "Exploring the Likelihood and Mechanism of a Climate-Change-Induced Dieback of the Amazon Rainforest," *Proceedings of the National Academy of Sciences*, special feature, published online February 13, 2009, www.pnas.org/content/ early/2009/02/12/0804619106.full.pdf+html?sid=70ec83be-9421 -4d09-a28e-4dd2584d2d77.

53. Woods Hole Research Center, "Forest Impacts of Our Artificial Drought," www.whrc.org/southamerica/drought_sim/results.htm.

54. Global Forest Expert Panel on Adaptation of Forests to Climate

Change, *Adaptation of Forests and People to Climate Change: A Global Assessment Report*, ed. Risto Seppälä, Alexander Buck, and Pia Katila, *World Series* 22 (Vienna: International Union of Forest Research Organizations, 2009). The report was published through an alliance of fourteen international organizations with substantial forestry programs called the Collaborative Partnership on Forests. You can download a PDF at www.iufro.org/science/gfep.

55. Hal Bernton, "Sea Life at Risk as Acid Levels Rise in Oceans," *The Seattle Times*, April 24, 2007.

56. R. E. Zeebel, J.C. Zachos, K. Caldeira, and T. Tyrrell, "Oceans: Carbon Emissions and Acidification," *Science* 321, no. 5885 (2008): 51–52.

57. S. Solomon, D. Qin, M. Manning, Z. Chen, M. Marquis, K. B. Averyt, M. Tignor, and H. L. Miller, eds., "IPCC 2007: Summary for Policymakers," in *Climate Change 2007: The Physical Science Basis. Contribution of Working Group I to the Fourth Assessment Report of the Intergovernmental Panel on Climate Change* (Cambridge, MA: Cambridge Univ. Press, 2007), 533–534.

58. John B. Miller, "Carbon Cycle: Sources, Sinks and Seasons," *Nature* 451, no. 7174 (January 3, 2008): 26–27.

59. Corinne Le Quéré, Christian Rödenbeck, Erik T. Buitenhuis, Thomas J. Conway, Ray Langenfelds, Antony Gomez, Casper Labuschagne, et al., "Saturation of the Southern Ocean CO_2 Sink Due to Recent Climate Change," *Science* 316, no. 5832 (May 17, 2007): 1735–1738.

60. Amanda Staudt, personal communication with author, April 1, 2009.

61. Susan Solomon, Gian-Kasper Plattner, Reto Knutti, and Pierre Friedlingstein, "Irreversible Climate Change Due to Carbon Dioxide Emissions," (lecture by Susan Solomon, National Academy of Sciences, Philadelphia, PA, January 28, 2009).

62. Richard Seager, Mingfang Ting, Isaac Held, Yochanan Kushnir, Jian Lu, Gabriel Vecchi, Huei-Ping Huang, et al., "Model Projections of an Imminent Transition to a More Arid Climate in Southwestern North America," *Science* 316, no. 5828 (2007): 1181–1184; and Solomon, "Irreversible Climate Change."

63. Kevin Anderson and Alice Bowes, "Reframing the Climate Change Challenge in Light of Post-2000 Emission Trends," *Phi. Trans. R. Soc. A.* 366, no. 1882 (November 2008): 3863–3882.

64. Isaiah 21:6.

65. Jared Diamond, *Collapse: How Societies Choose to Fail or Succeed* (New York: Viking, 2004).

1. Robert S. Boyd, "Glaciers Melting Worldwide, Study Finds," *Contra Costa Times* as reported by *National Geographic News*, August 21, 2002.

2. National Snow and Ice Data Center, "Global Glacier Recession," GLIMS Data at NSIDC, www.nsidc.org/glims/glaciermelt/index.html.

3. Lester R. Brown, *Plan B 3.0: Mobilizing to Save Civilization* (New York: W. W. Norton, 2008), 54.

4. Reuters, "China Drought Leaves 670,000 without Drinking Water," *ABC News*, April 13, 2008, www.abc.net.au/news/stories/2008/04/13/2215594.htm; "China's Tropical Province Sees Worsening Droughts," *China Daily*, January 16, 2008, www.chinadaily.com.cn/china/2008-01/16/content_6399572.htm.

5. Patty Glick, *Fish Out of Water: A Guide to Global Warming and Pacific Northwest Rivers* (Reston, VA: National Wildlife Federation, 2005).

6. This information came from a meeting with local officials during our July 2007 visit to Greenland.

7. "Greenland," introduction, Microsoft Encarta Online Encyclopedia 2009, http://encarta.msn.com/encyclopedia_761561107/Greenland.html.

8. Krishna Ramanujan, "Fastest Glacier in Greenland Doubles Speed," NASA, December 1, 2004, www.nasa.gov/vision/earth/lookingatearth/jakobshavn.html.

9. Cooperative Institute for Research in Environmental Sciences (CIRES), "Greenland Melt Accelerating, According to CU-Boulder Study," press release, December 11, 2007.

10. NASA, "Greenland Melt Accelerating: According to CU-Boulder Study," Earth Observatory, December 11, 2007. http://earthobservatory.nasa.gov/Newsroom/view.php?old=2007121126008.

11. Robert W. Corell, "Arctic Climate Impact Assessment" (statement before the Senate Committee on Commerce, Science and Transportation, March 3, 2004), www.groundtruthinvestigations.com/documents/climatechange.html.

12. CIRES, "Greenland Melt Accelerating."

13. Annette Varani, "Introducing Konrad Steffen," news and events, Cooperative Institute for Research in Environmental Sciences, Winter 2002, http://cires.colorado.edu/news/features/02/steffen.html.

14. CIRES, "Greenland Melt Accelerating."

15. MSNBC Online, "Record Ice Melt Seen on Greenland in 2007," December 11, 2007, www.msnbc.msn.com/id/22200767.

16. Seth Borenstein, "Ominous Arctic Melt Worries Experts," Associated Press, December 12, 2007, www.sanders.senate.gov/news/record.cfm ?id=288864.

17. CIRES, "Greenland Melt Accelerating."

18. Ibid.

19. NASA, "Scientists Detect Seasonal Patterns to Glacial Earthquakes in Greenland, See Signs of Increase," news, Earth Observatory, March 23, 2006, http://earthobservatory.nasa.gov/Newsroom/view .php?id=29757.

20. Explanation given by Professor Konrad Steffen during our July 2008 visit to Greenland.

21. G. Ekström, M. Nettles, and V. C. Tsai, "Seasonality and Increasing Frequency of Greenland Glacial Earthquakes," *Science* 311, no. 5768 (March 24, 2006): 1756–1758.

22. Göran Ekström has since transferred to Columbia University.

23. Ekström et al., "Seasonality and Increasing Frequency."

24. Johnny Rook, "The Ice Continues to Melt: Two Greenland Glaciers Breaking Up," *Daily Kos*, August 21, 2008, www.dailykos.com/story/ 2008/8/21/13753/4153/952/571629.

25. Associated Press, "Over 2T Tons of Ice Melted in Arctic since '03," ABC News, December 16, 2003, http://abcnews.go.com/Technology/ JustOneThing/wireStory?id=6469961.

26. Kendall Haven, "Greenland's Ice Island Alarm," feature article, Earth Observatory, August 28, 2007, http://earthobservatory.nasa.gov/ Study/Greenland/greenland5.html.

27. W. T. Pfeffer, J. T. Harper, and S. O'Neel, "Kinematic Constraints on Glacier Contributions to 21st-Century Sea-Level Rise," *Science* 321, no. 5894 (September 5, 2008): 1340–1334.

28. Haven, "Greenland's Ice Island Alarm."

29. Paul Brown, "Melting Ice Cap Triggering Earthquakes," *The Guardian* (London), September 8, 2007.

30. Michael W. Fincham, "A New Bay for the Oyster? Maryland Sea Grant," *Chesapeake Quarterly* 3, no. 3 (November 3, 2004).

31. National Oceanic and Atmospheric Administration, "Oyster Reefs: History," Restoration Portal, http://habitat.noaa.gov/restoration techniques/public/habitat.cfm?HabitatID=2&HabitatTopicID=10.

32. H. Bruce Franklin, "Net Losses: Declaring War on the Menhaden," *Mother Jones* (March/April 2006), www.motherjones.com/news/ feature/2006/03/net_losses.html.

33. Peter Stoler, "Rescuing a Protein Factory," *Time*, July 23, 1984.

34. Robert J. Nicholls, "Coastal Flooding and Wetland Loss in the 21st Century: Changes under the SRES Climate and Socio-economic Scenarios," *Global Environmental Change* 14, no. 1 (2004): 69–86.

35. Environmental Protection Agency, "Wetlands: Status and Trends," updated January 12, 2009, www.epa.gov/OWOW/wetlands/vital/status.html.

36. Nicholls, "Coastal Flooding."

37. National Wildlife Federation, "Global Warming and California," Western Climate Initiative, www.nwf.org/westernclimateinitiative/california.cfm.

38. Bob Marshall, "Last Chance: The Fight to Save a Disappearing Coast," *The Times-Picayune*, March 4, 2007.

39. Louisiana Wetland Protection Panel, *Saving Louisiana's Coastal Wetlands* (report, Louisiana Geological Survey and the EPA, April 1987), www.epa.gov/climatechange/effects/downloads/louisiana.pdf.

40. Donald F. Boesch, Russell B. Brinsfield, and Robert E. Magnien, "Chesapeake Bay Eutrophication Scientific Understanding, Ecosystem Restoration, and Challenges for Agriculture, Nutrient Management," *Journal of Environmental Quality* 30 (2001): 303–320.

41. Patty Glick, Amanda Staudt, and Brad Nunley, *Sea-Level Rise and Coastal Habitats of the Chesapeake Bay: A Summary* (report, National Wildlife Federation, 2008), www.nwf.org/sealevelrise/pdfs/NWF_ChesapeakeReportFINAL.pdf.

42. Robert Repetto, "The Climate Crisis and the Adaptation Myth" (working paper 13, Yale School of Forestry and Environmental Studies), 2, www.climateneeds.umd.edu/pdf/ClimateCrisisAdaptationMyth.pdf.

PART II: THE VICTIMS, THE PERPETRATORS, AND THE ENABLERS

CHAPTER 3: STRUGGLING SPECIES ARE FACING GLOBAL WARMING

1. The Native Fish Conservancy, "Update: The Hunt Is Off," www.nativefish.org/bluepike.

2. US Fish and Wildlife Service, "Endangered and Threatened Wildlife and Plants: Deregulation of the Longjaw Cisco and the Blue Pike," September 2, 1983 (48 FR 39941).

3. Sea lampreys were first observed in Lake Ontario in the 1830s. They did not invade Lake Erie prior to the "improvements" of the Welland Canal, made in 1919; sea lampreys were first observed in

Lake Erie in 1921, two years later. After spreading into Lake Erie, sea lampreys moved rapidly to the other Great Lakes. Great Lakes Fishery Commission, "Sea Lampreys: A Great Lakes Invader," Fact Sheet 3, www.glfc.org/pubs/FACT_3.pdf.

4. National Resources Conservation Service, *The Phosphorus Index: A Phosphorus Assessment Tool* (Washington, DC: US Department of Agriculture, August 1994), www.nrcs.usda.gov/technical/ECS/nutrient/pindex.html.

5. Phosphorus is in short supply and acts as the limiting nutrient in freshwater systems, while nitrogen is generally limiting in ocean environments.

6. Roger Knight and Phil Ryan, *Degradation of Fish Populations* (Lake Erie LaMP Technical Report No. 4, Lake Erie Lakewide Management Plan, October 1999), www.epa.gov/lakeerie/buia/lamp4.pdf.

7. American Fisheries Society, "Conservation Status of Imperiled North American Freshwater and Diadromous Fishes," *Fisheries* 13, no. 8 (August 2008): 372–407.

8. C. H. Marvin, S. Painter, M. N. Charlton, M. E. Fox, and P. A. Thiessen, "Trends in Spatial and Temporal Levels of Persistent Organic Pollutants in Lake Erie Sediments," *Chemosphere* 54: 33–40.

9. "Cuyahoga River Fire," Ohio History Central, July 1, 2005, www.ohiohistorycentral.org/entry.php?rec=1642.

10. University of Wisconsin Sea Grant Institute, "Round Goby," Fish of the Great Lakes, February 5, 2002, www.seagrant.wisc.edu/greatlakesfish/roundgoby.html; Timothy R. Johnson, David B. Bunnell, and Carey T. Knight, *A Potential New Energy Pathway in Central Lake Erie: The Round Goby Connection* (Ann Arbor, MI: International Association for Great Lakes Research, 2005).

11. V. A. Lee, "Factors Regulating Biomass and Contaminant Uptake by Round Gobies (*Neogobius melanostomus*) in Western Lake Erie" (master's thesis, University of Windsor, Windsor, Ontario, 2003).

12. T. B. Johnson, A. Allen, L. D. Corkum, and V. A. Lee, "Comparison of Methods Needed to Estimate Population Size of Round Gobies (*Neogobius melanostomus*) in Western Lake Erie" *Journal of Great Lakes Research* 31, no. 1 (2005): 78–86.

13. D. B. Bunnell, T. B. Johnson, and C. T. Knight, "The Impact of Introduced Round Gobies (*Neogobuis melanostomus*) on Phosphorus Cycling in Central Lake Erie," *Canadian Journal of Fisheries and Aquatic Sciences* 62 (2005): 15–29.

14. Hogan L. Southeward, E. Marcchall, C. Folt, R. A. Stein, "How Non-native Species in Lake Erie Influence Trophic Transfer of Mercury and Lead to Top Predators," *Journal of Great Lakes Research* 33 (2007): 46–61.

15. C. H. Marvin, S. Painter, and R. Rossmann, "Spatial and Temporal Patterns in Mercury Contamination in Sediments of the Laurentian Great Lakes," *Environmental Research* 95 (2004): 351–362.

16. J. H. Leach, "Biological Invasions of Lake Erie," *Point Pelee Natural History News* 1 (2001): 65–73.

17. Lake Erie Lakewide Management Plan (LaMP) Work Group, *Lake Erie LaMP 2008 Report* (updated coreport, Environment Canada and EPA, 2008), www.epa.gov/glnpo/lamp/le_2008/le_2008.pdf.

18. Barry Commoner, *The Closing Circle: Nature, Man and Technology* (New York: Alfred A. Knopf, 1971).

19. Stuart A. Ludsin, Mark W. Kershner, Karen A. Blocksom, Roger L. Knight, and Roy A. Stein, "Life after Death in Lake Erie: Nutrient Controls Drive Fish Species Richness, Rehabilitation," *Ecological Applications* 11, no. 3 (2001): 731–746.

20. Eric Chivian and Aaron Berstein, *Sustaining Life: How Human Health Depends on Biodiversity* (New York: Oxford Univ. Press, 2008), 38.

21. G. W. Kling, K. Hayhoe, L. B. Johnson, J. J. Magnuson, S. Polasky, S. K. Robinson, B. J. Shuter, et al., *Confronting Climate Change in the Great Lakes Region: Impacts on our Communities and Ecosystems* (Cambridge, MA: Union of Concerned Scientists; and Washington, DC: Ecological Society of America; 2003), 69.

22. Raymond A. Assel, *Lake Erie Ice Cover Climatology: Basin Averaged Ice Cover: Winters 1898–2002* (Ann Arbor, MI: Great Lakes Environmental Research Laboratory, Contribution No. 1309, 2004).

23. Boddu N. Venkatesh and Benjamin F. Hobbs, "Analyzing Investments for Managing Lake Erie Levels under Climate Change Uncertainty," *Water Resources Research* 35, no. 5 (May 1999).

24. LaMP Work Group, *Lake Erie LaMP 2008 Report.*

CHAPTER 4: ON THIN ICE

1. Eva Terese Jenssen, "Spectacular Find Could Rewrite Polar Bear History," University Centre in Svalbard, December 17, 2007, www.unis.no/60_NEWS/6030_Archive_2007/n_17_12_07_polarbear_jawbone/polarbear_jawbone_news_17122007.htm.

2. "Polar Bears: Adaptations for an Aquatic Environment," Sea World/

Busch Gardens Animal Information Database, May 16, 2009. www
.seaworld.org/animal-info/info-books/polar-bear/adaptations.htm.

3. I. Sterling and D. Guravich, *Polar Bears* (Ann Arbor: Univ. of Michigan Press, 1988), 113–136.

4. Conversation with guides attending the Canadian Wildlife Federation annual meeting, May 31, 2007.

5. Dan Joling, "9 Polar Bears Observed on Risky Open Ocean Swims," ABC News, August 21, 2008, http://abcnews.go.com/Technology/ wireStory?id=5630053.

6. Associated Press, "Polar Bear Sightings Stir Climate Debate," *Los Angeles Times*, August 22, 2008.

7. Andrew E. Derocher, "Polar Bears in a Warming Arctic," in *Sudden and Disruptive Climate Change: Exploring the Real Risks and How We Can Avoid Them*, ed. Michael C. MacCracken, Frances Moore, and John C. Toppings Jr. (London: Earthscan Publications, 2008), 199.

8. Jon Aars, Nicholas J. Lunn, and Andrew E. Derocher, *Polar Bears: Proceedings of the 14th Working Meeting of the IUCN/SSC Polar* (Gland, Switzerland: International Union for the Conservation of Nature, 2006).

9. Eric V. Regehr, Steven C. Amstrup, and Ian Stirling, "Polar Bear Population Status in the Southern Beaufort Sea," Open-File Report 2006-1337, US Department of the Interior, US Geological Survey, 2006, http://pubs.usgs.gov/of/2006/1337/pdf/ofr20061337.pdf.

10. Aars et al., *Polar Bears.*

11. Arctic National Wildlife Refuge, "Historical Timeline of the Polar Bear ESA Listing," 2007, www.anwr.org/archives/historical_timeline_of _the_polar_bear_esa_listing.php.

12. "Interior Secretary Kempthorne Announces Proposal to List Polar Bears as Threatened Under Endangered Species Act," press release, Department of the Interior, December 27, 2006.

13. Sarah Palin, "Bearing Up," op-ed, *The New York Times*, January 5, 2008.

14. State of Alaska, "Alaska to Sue Over Polar Bear Listing: Seeking to Overturn Decision," News and Announcements, no. 08-134, www .gov.state.ak.us/news.php?id=1383.

15. Tom Kizzi, "E-mail Reveals State Dispute over Polar Bear Listing: Biologists Disagreed with Administration," *Anchorage Daily News*, May 25, 2008.

16. Jonathan Amos, "Arctic Summers Ice-free 'by 2013,'" BBC News,

December 12, 2007, http://news.bbc.co.uk/2/hi/science/nature/7139797.stm.

CHAPTER 5: THE GREATEST SHOW ON EARTH

1. Thomas E. Lovejoy, Lee Hannah, eds., "A 'Paleoperspective' on Climate Variability and Change," in *Change and Biodiversity* (New Haven, CT: Yale Univ. Press, 2004), 89, 91.

2. Ecological Research and Development Group, "The Horseshoe Crab: Spawning," www.horseshoecrab.org/nh/spawn.html.

3. The horseshoe crab, considered a living fossil, is closely related to trilobites dating as far back as 544 million years ago, which we find only in fossils.

4. Leah Barash, "Mass Appeal," *National Wildlife Magazine* 31, no. 4 (June/July 1993), www.nwf.org/nationalwildlife/printerFriendly.cfm?issueID=96&articleID=1279.

5. "Red knot, *Calidris canutus rufa*, Northeast Region," US Fish and Wildlife Service, 1, www.fws.gov/northeast/redknot/facts.pdf.

6. Daniel K. Niven and Gregory S. Butcher, *Northward Shifts in the Abundance of North American Birds in Early Winter: A Response to Warmer Winter Temperatures?* (New York: Audubon, 2009), www.audubon.org/news/pressroom/bacc/pdfs/Report.pdf.

7. Jeffery E. Lovich, "Turtles and Global Climate Change," USGS, November 25, 2003, http://geochange.er.usgs.gov/sw/impacts/biology/turtles.

8. Gina Hayes, "An Introduction to Sea Turtles: Evolution and Comparison of Leatherbacks, Loggerheads, Greens and Hawksbills," *TME* (June 2005), http://jrscience.wcp.muohio.edu/fieldcourses05/PapersMarineEcologyArticles/AnIntroductiontoSeaTurtle.html.

9. K. J. Long and B. A. Schroeder, eds., *Proceedings of the International Technical Expert Workshop on Marine Turtle Bycatch in Longline Fisheries* (NOAA technical memorandum NMFS-F/OPR-26, US Dept. of Commerce, 2004), 4, www.nmfs.noaa.gov/pr/pdfs/interactions/turtle_bycatch_workshop.pdf.

10. Marti L. McCracken, *Estimation of Sea Turtle Take and Mortality in the Hawaiian Longline Fisheries* (Honolulu: Southwest Fisheries Science Center, 2000).

11. Jeffrey J. Polovina, Evan Howell, Denise M. Parker, and George H. Balazs, "Dive-depth distribution of loggerhead (*Carretta carretta*) and olive ridley (*Lepidochelys olivacea*) sea turtles in the central North

Pacific: Might deep longline sets catch fewer turtles?" *Fish. Bull.* 101, no. 1 (2003): 189–193.

12. *Aboriginal Law Bulletin*, "Mohawks Make General Motors Pay," www .austlii.edu.au/au/journals/AboriginalLB/1986/5.html.

13. US Geological Survey, "Biological and Ecotoxicological Characteristics of Terrestrial Vertebrate Species Residing in Estuaries," www.pwrc .usgs.gov/bioeco/snturtle.htm.

14. National Institute of Standards and Technology, "Sea Turtle Health Linked to Contaminants," *ScienceDaily*, May 11, 2004, www .sciencedaily.com/releases/2004/05/040510014420.htm.

15. "Climate Change and Sea Turtles," Global Warming, www.global -greenhouse-warming.com/climate-change-and-sea-turtles.html.

16. M. C. Wicklow-Howard, *Vesicular-Arbusculab Mycorrhizae from Sagebrush Steppe Habitat in Western Idaho and Central Oregon* (Boise, ID: Boise State Univ., 1994), www.icbemp.gov/science/wicklow1.pdf.

17. David Stauth, "Study: Vast Sagebrush Ecosystems a Victim of Climate Change?" Oregon State University News and Communication Services, August 29, 2005, http://oregonstate.edu/dept/ncs/newsarch/2005/ Aug05/sagebrush.htm.

18. Robert S. Thompson, Steven W. Hostetler, Patrick J. Bartlein, and Katherine H. Anderson, *A Strategy for Assessing Potential Future Changes in Climate, Hydrology, and Vegetation in the Western United States*, (circular 1153, Washington, DC: US Geological Survey, 1998).

19. J. D. Yoakum and B. W. O'Gara, *Pronghorn, Ecology and Management of Large Mammals in North America*, ed. Stephen Demarais and Paul R. Krausman (Upper Saddle River, NJ: Prentice Hall, 2000), 559–577.

20. Associated Press, "Study: Pronghorn Thrive in Wolves' Shadow," *USA Today*, March, 3, 2008; Wildlife Conservation Society, "Are Wolves the Pronghorn's Best Friend?" *ScienceDaily*, March 4, 2008, www .sciencedaily.com/releases/2008/03/080303145300.htm.

21. David E. Brown, Dana Warnecke, and Ted McKinney, "Effects of Midsummer Drought on Mortality of Doe Pronghorn," *The Southwestern Naturalist* 51, no. 2 (2006): 220–225.

22. Nevada Cooperative Extension and Bureau of Land Management Nevada Office, "Be Careful! Cheatgrass Is Extremely Flammable! 2005 Is a Record Year for Cheatgrass Growth in Nevada," www .wildfirelessons.net/documents/Cheatgrass_flyer_final.pdf.

23. Patty Glick, *Fueling the Fire: Global Warming, Fossil Fuels and the Fish and Wildlife of the American West* (Reston, VA: National Wildlife

Federation, October 2006), www.nwf.org/globalwarming/pdfs/Fuel
ingTheFire.pdf.

24. John Roach, "By 2050 Warming to Doom Million Species, Study
Says," *National Geographic News*, July 12, 2004, http://news
.nationalgeographic.com/news/2004/01/0107_040107_extinction.html.

25. Thomas E. Lovejoy, Lee Hannah, eds., "Introduction," in *Change and
Biodiversity* (New Haven, CT: Yale Univ. Press, 2004), 4.

26. Donald Worster, *Dust Bowl: The Southern Plains in the 1930s* (New
York: Oxford Univ. Press, 1979), 11–12.

27. A. Fischlin, G. F. Midgley, J. T. Price, R. Leemans, B. Gopal, C. Turley,
M. D. A. Rounsevell, et al., "Ecosystems, Their Properties, Goods,
and Services," in *Climate Change 2007: Impacts, Adaptation and
Vulnerability*, ed. M. L. Parry, O.F. Canziani, J. P. Palutikof, P. J. van
der Linden, and C. E. Hanson (Cambridge: Cambridge Univ. Press,
2007), 211–272.

28. Jay R. Malcolm, Canran Liu, Ronald P. Neilson, Lara Hansen, and
Lee Hannah, "Global Warming and Extinctions of Endemic Species
from Biodiversity Hotspots," *Conservation Biology* 20, no. 2 (2006),
538–548.

29. Chris D. Thomas, Alison Cameron, Rhys E. Green, Michael Bakkenes,
Linda J. Beaumont, Yvonne C. Collingham, Barend F. N. Erasmus,
et al., "Extinction Risk from Climate Change," *Nature* 427, no. 6970
(January 2004): 145–148.

30 J. M. Scott, B. Griffith, R. S. Adamcik, D. M. Ashe, B. Czech, R. L.
Fischman, P. Gonzalez, et al., "2008: National Wildlife Refuges,"
chapter 5 in *Preliminary Review of Adaptation Options for
Climate-Sensitive Ecosystems and Resources* (Washington, DC: US
Environmental Protection Agency, 5–17.

31. Stavros Dimas, in the foreword to *The Economics of Ecosystems and
Biodiversity: An Interim Report* by Pavan Sukhdev (n.p.: European
Communities, 2008), 3. http://ec.europa.eu/environment/nature/
biodiversity/economics/pdf/teeb_report.pdf.

CHAPTER 6: IN THE ABSENCE OF LIGHT

1. "Runaway Climate Change? Massive Methane Release off Siberia?
Nah, Let's Talk about Wall Street Instead!" blog entry at Thoughts on
Climate Change: A Canadian Perspective, September 30, 2008, http://
climatechangecdn.blogspot.com/2008/09/runaway-climate-change
-massive-methane.html.

2. James Hansen, "Twenty Years Later: Tipping Points Near on Global Warming," *The Guardian* (London), June 23, 2008, www.guardian .co.uk/environment/2008/jun/23/climatechange.carbonemissions.

3. Al Gore, *The Assault on Reason* (New York: Penguin, 2007), 3.

4. K. M. Walter, S. A. Zimov, J. P. Chanton, D. Verbyla, and F. S. Chapin, "Methane Bubbling from Siberian Thaw Lakes as a Positive Feedback to Climate Warming," *Nature* 443, no. 7107 (September 7, 2006): 71–75.

5. Gavin Schmidt, "Methane: A Scientific Journey from Obscurity to Climate Super-Stardom," Goddard Institute for Space Studies, September 2004, www.giss.nasa.gov/research/features/methane.

6. Jonathan Amos, "Arctic Summers Ice-free 'by 2013,'" BBC News, December 12, 2007, http://news.bbc.co.uk/2/hi/science/ nature/7139797.stm.

7. Danny Schechter, "Dung on All Their Houses," *Toward Freedom*, December/January 2000, www.thirdworldtraveler.com/Media_con trol_propaganda/Dung_Houses.html.

8. Curtis Brainard, "ABC Declines Renewable Power Ad: Gore's Alliance for Climate Protection Launches Petition," The Observatory, *Columbia Journalism Review*, October 10, 2008, www.cjr.org/the_observatory/ abc_declines_renewable_power_a.php.

9. Eoin O'Carroll, "Why Won't ABC Air That Clean-energy Ad?" Bright Green Blog, *The Christian Science Monitor*, October 10, 2008, http:// features.csmonitor.com/environment/2008/10/10/why-wont-abc-air -that-clean-energy-ad.

10. Simon Leufstedt, "ABC Refuses to Run Ad That Attacks Big Oil," blog posting, October 10, 2008, GreenBlog.com, www.green-blog .org/2008/10/10/abc-refuses-to-run-ad-that-attacks-big-oil/#more-538.

11. Peter O'Neil, "Poll: Efforts to Support Global Climate-change Falls," *The Windsor Star*, November 27, 2008.

12. Sourcewatch, "American Coalition for Clean Coal Electricity," May 5, 2009, www.sourcewatch.org/index.php?title=American_Coalition _for_Clean_Coal_Electricity.

13. Gülbin Gürdal, "Geochemistry of Trace Elements in Çan Coal (Miocene), Çanakkale, Turkey" (paper, Mart University Engineering and Architecture Faculty, Department of Geological Engineering, Çanakkale, Turkey, 2007).

14. Lee B. Clarkea, "The Fate of Trace Elements during Coal Combustion and Gasification: An Overview" (paper, Coal Research, London, 2003).

15. J. P. McBride, R. E. Moore, J. P. Witherspoon, and R. E. Blanco,

"Radiological Impact of Airborne Effluents of Coal and Nuclear Plants," *Science* 202, no. 4372 (December 8, 1978): 1045–1050.

16. National Council on Radiation Protection and Measurements, "Public Radiation Exposure from Nuclear Power Generation in the United States" *Reports* no. 92 (1987), www.ncrppublications.org/index.cfm?fm=Product.AddToCart&pid=3874478138 and no. 95, "Radiation Exposure of the U.S. Population from Consumer Products and Miscellaneous Sources" (1987), www.ncrppublications.org/index.cfm?fm=Product.AddToCart&pid=8607600177.

17. Jane Hightower, "A Call for Tougher Standards on Mercury Levels in Fish: An Opinion," *Yale Environment 360*, January 26, 2009, www.e360.yale.edu/content/feature.msp?id=2113.

18. "Study Links Autism Risk to Distance from Power Plants," *HLC News* 41, no. 9 (May 08, 2008). www.uthscsa.edu/hscnews/singleformat.asp?newID=2739.

19. Autism Society of America, prevalence statistics from Centers for Disease Control and Prevention (2007 and 2001) and 2000 US Census figures; costs are extrapolations from K. Jarbrink and M. Knapp, "The Economic Impact on Autism in Britain," *Autism* 5, no. 1 (2001): 7–22, www.autism-society.org/site/PageServer?pagename=about_whatis_factsstats.

20. EPA, "Notice of Data Availability on the Disposal of Coal Combustion Wastes in Landfills and Surface Impoundments," *Federal Register* 72, no. 167 (August 29, 2007), 49714–49719.

21. Business Wire, "ACCCE Statement Regarding Proposed Oregon State Climate Agenda," October 28, 2008, www.thefreelibrary.com/ACCCE+Statement+Regarding+Proposed+Oregon+State+Climate+Agenda.-a0187928818.

22. The Reality Campaign website is www.thisisreality.org.

23. Bob Norman, "Newspaper Layoffs, Partnerships, and the Net Conspire to Kill South Florida's Dailies," *Miami New Times News*, October 29, 2008.

24. Deborah Potter, "Pessimism Rules in TV Newsrooms," Journalism.org, November 1, 2002, http://journalism.org/node/226.

25. From the Society of Professional Journalists' Code of Ethics, available at www.spj.org/ethicscode.asp.

26. Larry J. Schweiger, "Looking North, Seeing Our Future," *National Wildlife* 43 no. 3, (April/May 2005), www.nwf.org/NationalWildlife/article.cfm?issueID=74&articleID=1051.

27. Glenn Beck, "Exposed: The Climate of Fear," transcript, CNN News, May 2, 2007, http://transcripts.cnn.com/TRANSCRIPTS/0705/02/gb.01.html.

28. "NASA Study Links Severe Storm Increases, Global Warming," ScienceDaily, December 28, 2008, www.sciencedaily.com/releases/2008/12/081227214927.htm.

29. "Global Warming Equals Stronger Hurricanes, Meteorologists Find That Increased Ocean Temperatures Cause Increasingly Intense Hurricanes," ScienceDaily, February 1, 2008, www.sciencedaily.com/videos/2008/0204-global_warming_equals_stronger_hurricanes.htm.

30. Sharon Begley, "Global Warming Is a Cause of This Year's Extreme Weather," Technology True or False, *Newsweek*, July 7, 2008.

31. Michael J. de la Merced, "Weather Channel Is Sold to NBC and Equity Firms," *The New York Times*, July 7, 2008.

32. Andrew Freedman, "NBC Fires Weather Channel Environmental Unit, Some On-camera Meteorologists Also Let Go," *The Washington Post*, November 21, 2008.

33. Rush Limbaugh, "Stack of Stuff Quick Hits Page Story #3: NBC Fires Politicized Weather Channel Staff," November 24, 2008, www.rushlimbaugh.com/home/daily/site_112408/content/01125104.guest.html.

34. To learn more about who owns what, visit the *Columbia Journalism Review* at www.cjr.org/resources/index.php?c=index.

PART III: TIME FOR RENEWAL AND IMMEDIATE ACTION

CHAPTER 7: RENEWING, RECHARGING, AND REBUILDING AMERICA

Epigraph. Thomas Valone, *Harnessing the Wheelwork of Nature: Tesla's Science of Energy* (Kempton, IL: Adventures Unlimited Press, 2002), 45.

1. US Department of Energy Office of Energy Efficiency and Renewable Energy, "Energy Efficiency Trends in Residential and Commercial Buildings," October 2008, 4, http://apps1.eere.energy.gov/buildings/publications/pdfs/corporate/bt_stateindustry.pdf.

2. Ibid.

3. Ibid., 9.

4. Van Jones, *The Green Collar Economy: How One Solution Can Fix Our Two Biggest Problems* (New York: HarperCollins, 2008), 9.

5. Architecture 2030, "Face It: There Is a Solution to Global Warming,"

press release, January 4, 2008, www.architecture2030.org/news/articles/2030_ReverberateCampaign.pdf.

6. The 2030 Challenge is available at www.architecture2030.org/2030_challenge/index.html.

7. Ed Mazria, founder, Architecture 2030, from e-mail to author on December 23, 2008. For more information, see Architecture 2030 at www.architecture2030.org.

8. Ed Mazria, e-mail to author, December 23, 2008.

9. Reid Detchon and Bracken Hendricks, "Rebuilding America and Creating Green Jobs," (unpublished paper, Energy Future Coalition and Center for American Progress, November 25, 2008).

10. "Transcript: Obama's Speech to Congress," CBS News, February 24, 2009, www.cbsnews.com/stories/2009/02/24/politics/main4826494.shtml.

11. Glenn Hunter, "GM's Lutz on Hybrids, Global Warming, and Cars as Art," *D Magazine*, January 30, 2008, http://frontburner.dmagazine.com/2008/01/30/gms-lutz-on-hybrids-global-warming-and-cars-as-art.

12. David Welch, "GM's Latest Challenge: Losing Lutz," *Business Week*, February 9, 2009.

13. General Motors Corporation, *2009–2014 Restructuring Plan* (Detroit, MI: General Motors Corp., February 17, 2009), http://preprodha.ecomm.gm.com:8221/us/gm/en/news/govt/docs/plan.pdf.

14. Tesla Motors, "Charging and Batteries," www.teslamotors.com/efficiency/how_it_works.php.

15. Tesla Motors, "The Battery," www.teslamotors.com/efficiency/charging_and_batteries.php.

16. William Clay Ford, "New Mobility Means Business: Emerging Markets in Sustainable Urban Transportation" (presentation at SMART Conference "New Mobility: The Emerging Transportation Economy," June 11, 2008), http://um-smart.org/resources/conference/video.html.

17. Timothy Searchinger, Ralph Heimlich, R. A. Houghton, Fengxia Dong, Amani Elobeid, Jacinto Fabiosa, Simla Tokgoz, et al., "Use of U.S. Croplands for Biofuels Increases Greenhouse Gases through Emissions from Land Use Change," *Science* 319, no. 5867 (February 29, 2008).

18. More information on the International Biochar Initiative is available at www.biochar-international.org.

19. Spencer Abraham, *National Transmission Grid Study* (report, US Department of Energy, May 2002), www.pi.energy.gov/documents/TransmissionGrid.pdf.

20. Ken Zweibel, James Mason, and Vasilis Fthenakis, "A Solar Grand Plan: By 2050 Solar Power Could End U.S. Dependence on Foreign Oil and Slash Greenhouse Gas Emissions," *Scientific American*, January 2008.

21. Private letter to author, dated January 2, 2009.

22. Greg Allen, "U.S. Gives Nuclear Power a Second Look," *Morning Edition*, NPR, March 28, 2008, www.npr.org/templates/story/story.php?storyId=89169837.

23. Todd Woody, "Wind Jobs Outstrip the Coal Industry," *Fortune*, January 28, 2009.

24. These attitudes and intentions are apparent at www.EnergyTomorrow.com.

25. Marianne Lavelle, "Gore Business: 2340 Climate Lobbyists," Politico, February 25, 2009, www.politico.com/news/stories/0209/19255.html.

26. John P. Holdren, "Meeting the Climate-Change Challenge" (eighth annual John H. Chafee memorial lecture on science and the environment, National Council for Science and the Environment, Washington, DC, January 17, 2008).

27. "Barack Obama and Joe Biden: New Energy for America," factsheet, Obama for America, www.barackobama.com/pdf/factsheet_energy_speech_080308.pdf.

28. President Barack Obama, "Remarks of President Barack Obama: Address to Joint Session of Congress" (address to joint session of Congress, Washington, DC, February 24, 2009).

29. Jan Lopatka, "Obama Says to Take Lead on Climate, EU Pleased," Reuters, April 5, 2009, www.reuters.com/article/latestCrisis/idUSL5180795.

CHAPTER 8: PUTTING THE BLACK BACK IN OUR SOILS

1. News staff, "Soil More at Risk from Climate Change Than Air Is," Scientific Blogging, November 24, 2008, www.scientificblogging.com/news_releases/soil_more_risk_climate_change_air.

2. James E. Hansen, "Political Interference with Government Climate Change Science" (testimony to Committee on Oversight and Government Reform, United States House of Representatives, March 19, 2007), 10.

3. J. Hansen, Mki. Sato, P. Kharecha, D. Beerling, R. Berner, V. Masson-Delmotte, M. Pagani, et al., "Target atmospheric CO_2: Where Should Humanity Aim?" *Open Atmospheric Science Journal* 2 (2008): 217–231.

CHAPTER 9: THE ROLE OF ENVIRONMENTAL EDUCATION

1. Michael Jamison, "Boiling Point: Heat Causes Big Fish Kill Near Kalispell," *Missoulian*, July 25, 2007; David Quammen, "Jeremy Bentham, the Pieta, and a Precious Few Grayling," Audubon, May 1982, www.nativefish.org/articles/grayling.php.

2. National Wildlife Federation, *National Opinion Survey of Hunters and Anglers* (Harrisonburg, VA: Responsive Management, March/April 2006), www.targetglobalwarming.org/files/Toplines_National_FINAL.pdf.

3. Ibid. More than 40 million Americans hunt and fish, and they generated some $75 billion in annual expenditures from their activities in 2006 alone. Nationwide, approximately one out of every five eligible voters is a hunter or angler. The poll had a sampling error of +/- 3.05 percent at a 95 percent confidence level.

4. "Global Warming: A Divide on Causes and Solutions: Public Views Unchanged by Unusual Weather," poll, Pew Research Center for the People & the Press, January 24, 2007, http://pewresearch.org/pubs/282/global-warming-a-divide-on-causes-and-solutions.

5. National Wildlife Federation, *National Opinion Survey*.

6. James M. Jasper, *Restless Nation: Starting Over in America* (Univ. of Chicago Press, 2000).

7. Susan S. Lang, "Camping, Hiking, and Fishing in the Wild as a Child Breeds Respect for Environment in Adults, Study Finds," Chronicle Online, March 13, 2006, www.news.cornell.edu/stories/March06/wild.nature.play.ssl.html.

8. *Outdoor Recreation Participation Report 2008* (Boulder, CO: Outdoor Foundation, 2008), 2, www.outdoorfoundation.org/research.participation.2008.html.

9. Rhonda Clements, "An Investigation of the Status of Outdoor Play," *Contemporary Issues in Early Childhood* 5, no. 1 (2004), 72.

10. Joe L. Frost, "The Dissolution of Children's Outdoor Play: Causes and Consequences," *Early Childhood Education Journal* 29 (May 11, 2006), 111–117.

11. Kaiser Family Foundation, "Media Multi-Tasking Changing the Amount and Nature of Young People's Media Use," news release,

Kaiser Family Foundation, March 9, 2005.

12. O. Bartosh, M. Tudor, C. Taylor, and L. Ferguson, "Improving WASL Scores through Environmental Education: Is It Possible?" *Applied Environmental Education and Communication* 5, no. 3 (2006).

13. Romina M. Barros, Ellen J. Silver, and Ruth E. K. Stein, "School Recess and Group Classroom Behavior," *Pediatrics* 123, no. 2 (February 2009): 431–436.

14. Kaiser Family Foundation, "Media Multi-Tasking."

15. W. Dietz, "Physical Activity Recommendations: Where Do We Go from Here?" *The Journal of Pediatrics* 146, no. 6: 719–720.

16. Stanford University, *Building 'Generation Play': Addressing the Crisis of Inactivity among America's Children* (report, Stanford Prevention Research Center, Stanford University School of Medicine, February 2007), www.playeveryday.org/Stanford%20Report.pdf.

17. Centers for Disease Control and Prevention, "Guidelines for School and Community Programs to Promote Lifelong Physical Activity among Young People," *Morbidity and Mortality Weekly Reports* 46, no. RR-6, 1–36, www.kidsource.com/kidsource/content4/promote.phyed.html.

18. RoperASW, *Outdoor Recreation in America 2003: Recreation's Benefits to Society Challenged by Trends* (report for the Recreation Roundtable, January 2004), www.funoutdoors.com/files/ROPER%20REPORT%202004_0.pdf.

19. Rachel Carson, *A Sense of Wonder* (New York: Harper & Row, 1965), 42–45.

20. René Dubos, "The Limits of Adaptability," in *The Environmental Handbook* by Garret De Bell (New York: Ballantine Books, 1970), 27.

21. Aldo Leopold, "The Conservation Ethic," *Journal of Forestry* 31 (October 1933): 634–643.

22. Edward O. Wilson, *The Diversity of Life* (New York: W. W. Norton, 1999), 351.

23. Adapted from a presentation by Larry Schweiger, "Preserving Past Traditions, Creating New Connections" (lecture, Pennsylvania Governors Outdoor Conference, State College, PA, March 19, 2007), www.connectoutdoors.state.pa.us/PROCEEDINGS.ASPX.

CHAPTER 10: LAST CHANCE

1. Susan Solomon, Gian-Kasper Plattnerb, Reto Knuttic, and Pierre Friedlingsteind, "Irreversible Climate Change Due to Carbon

Dioxide Emissions," *Proceedings of the National Academy of Sciences* 106, no. 6 (December 16, 2008): 1704–1709, www.pnas.org/content/early/2009/01/28/0812721106.abstract?sid=1e8d9043-4f99-4176-9d38-7be0f3540a28.

2. Richard Harris, "Global Warming Is Irreversible, Study Says," *All Things Considered*, NPR, January 26, 2009.

3. Ralph Abele, "The Straight 'Talk Years'" in *The One Who Insists* (Harrisburg, PA: Ralph W. Abele Conservation Scholarship Fund, 1987).

4. Rachel Carson, *Silent Spring* (Boston: Riverside Press, 1962), 16.

5. The eight Republican US Representatives who voted in favor of the American Clean Energy and Security Act of 2009 on June 26, 2009, were Reps. Bono Mack (CA), Castle (DE), Kirk (IL), Lanie (NJ), LoBiondo (NJ), McHugh (NY), Reichert (WA), and C. Smith (NJ).

6. Riley E. Dunlap, "Climate-Change Views: Republican-Democratic Gaps Expand," Gallup.com, May 29, 2008, www.gallup.com/poll/107569/ClimateChange-Views-RepublicanDemocratic-Gaps-Expand.aspx.

7. Thomas S. Kuhn, *The Structure of Scientific Revolutions* (Chicago: Univ. of Chicago Press, 1962).

8. Roberta Combs, speech at the National Wildlife Federation Convention, Pittsburgh, PA, May 1, 2009.

9. An expression taken from the title of a book by Charles E. Hummel, *Tyranny of the Urgent* (Downers Grove, IL: Intervarsity Press, 1967).

FURTHER READING AND ACTION

For those who want to learn more about specific subjects covered in this book, I have prepared a list of books for further reading. This is not intended to be an exhaustive list, as there are many fine books on the various subjects.

I also highly recommend reading the Fourth IPCC report in its entirety (found online at www.ipcc.ch/ipccreports/ar4 -syr.htm) and a report recently released by the US Global Change Research Program that summarizes climate changes and impacts already observed in the United States and that makes clear that the decisions we make now about reducing emissions will determine the severity of climate change impacts going forward. The report can be found at www.global change.gov/usimpacts.

To take action today, the National Wildlife Federation's primary online source of climate information is constantly updated at www.nwf.org/globalwarming. And of course, I highly recommend exploring the many other online references listed in the sidebars and cited in the notes section. In the world of science, new data and reports appear almost daily, so the Internet is an extremely important tool for keeping up with new information about climate change.

Part II: The Victims, the Perpetrators, and the Enablers

Chapter 3: Struggling Ecosystems Are Facing Global Warming
Climate Change and Biodiversity
> Thomas E. Lovejoy and Lee Hannah

> The name Tom Lovejoy and biodiversity are nearly synonymous. This is a readable scientific assessment of climate and its impact on biodiversity.

Chapter 4: On Thin Ice
Frozen Oceans: The Floating World of Pack Ice
> David N. Thomas

> This book looks at pack ice in an introductory, exploratory way but does not detail the more recent declines in the Arctic.

Heatstroke: Nature in an Age of Global Warming
> Anthony Barnosky

Chapter 5: The Greatest Show on Earth
Sustaining Life: How Human Health Depends on Biodiversity
> Eric Chivian and Aaron Bernstein

> For anyone who doubts that humanity needs to protect nature, this book, involving over one hundred scientists, links biodiversity to human health. It reveals amazing and comprehensive stories about how much of our food and medicines come from nature.

Chapter 6: In the Absence of Light
The Assault on Reason
> Al Gore

> As a former newspaper journalist, Gore has been a leader in advancing the digital age of information. He provides a compelling story of what is happening to journalism in America.

The Revolution Will Not Be Televised: Democracy, the Internet,
and the Overthrow of Everything
   Joe Trippi

   Trippi's book accurately predicts the revolution that has become
   the new foundation for modern elections in America, starting with
   President Barack Obama.

The New Geography: How the Digital Revolution Is Reshaping the
American Landscape
   Joel Kotkin

PART III: TIME FOR RENEWAL AND IMMEDIATE ACTION

CHAPTER 7: RENEWING, RECHARGING, AND REBUILDING AMERICA
Our Choice
   Al Gore

   Our Choice will be published November 3, 2009. This book promises
   to give great hope for new solutions. In preparing for the writing, Gore
   met with many of the most innovative people on the planet. For details,
   go to the link on Al Gore's blog describing the book: http://blog.algore
   .com/2009/03/our_choice.html.

Earth: The Sequel: The Race to Reinvent Energy and Stop Global Warming
   Fred Krupp and Miriam Horn

   This book explores the growing opportunity for innovation leading to
   technical and efficiency solutions to global warming.

The Green Collar Economy: How One Solution Can Fix
Our Two Biggest Problems
   Van Jones

   Jones has made it clear that we must look for inclusive solutions to
   global warming that give jobs and hope to urban, largely minority
   communities.

For the Common Good: Redirecting the Economy toward Community,
the Environment, and a Sustainable Future
   Herman E. Daly and John B. Cobb Jr.

   For those who want to look at economics from an ecologically sustainable vantage point, this is the seminal work.

Beyond Growth: The Economics of Sustainable Development
   Herman E. Daly

   This is an excellent resource on sustainable economic development.

CHAPTER 8: PUTTING THE BLACK BACK IN OUR SOILS

Soil Carbon Management: Economic, Environmental, and Societal Benefits
   John M. Kimble et al.

   This and the following title are both technical reference books on the subject.

Assessment Methods for Soil Carbon
   John M. Kimble et al.

CHAPTER 9: THE ROLE OF ENVIRONMENTAL EDUCATION

Earth-Wise: A Biblical Response to Environmental Issues
   Calvin B. DeWitt

   DeWitt is the progenitor of the modern creation-care movement in America. He has been a pioneer and a true inspiration for those who connect their faith with stewardship.

Last Child in the Woods
   Richard Louv

   As the publisher of *Ranger Rick*, *Your Big Backyard*, and *Wild Animal Babies*, the NWF has long been committed to reaching children and connecting them to nature. Louv has made an important case for why this is so important. We are indebted to him for helping us to understand "nature deficit disorder."

Chapter 10: Last Chance

Visit my blog at www.nwf.org/view to learn how you can get involved in the legislative efforts to avoid the climate crisis and stay informed about recent developments in science and policy.

Earth in the Balance: Ecology and the Human Spirit
Al Gore

With amazing foresight, this is Gore's first attempt to get our attention, and it speaks to a new way forward.

Fighting for Love in the Century of Extinction: How Passion and Politics Can Stop Global Warming
Eban Goodstein

Goldstein, a passionate college professor, has been energizing college students on over eight hundred campuses to learn the truth through his "Teach In" and other calls to take action.

Index

green press

INITIATIVE

Fulcrum Publishing is committed to preserving ancient forests and natural resources. We elected to print this title on 100% postconsumer recycled paper, processed chlorine-free. As a result, we have saved:

107 Trees (40' tall and 6-8" diameter)
34 Million BTUs of Total Energy
10,126 Pounds of Greenhouse Gases
48,769 Gallons of Wastewater
2,961 Pounds of Solid Waste

Fulcrum Publishing made this paper choice because our printer, Thomson-Shore, Inc., is a member of Green Press Initiative, a nonprofit program dedicated to supporting authors, publishers, and suppliers in their efforts to reduce their use of fiber obtained from endangered forests.

For more information, visit www.greenpressinitiative.org

Environmental impact estimates were made using the Environmental Defense Paper Calculator. For more information visit: www.edf.org/papercalculator

For a complete list of all titles in the Speaker's Corner series
and to order a catalog of our books, please contact us at:

 FULCRUM PUBLISHING

4690 Table Mountain Drive, Suite 100
Golden, Colorado 80403
E-mail: info@fulcrumbooks.com
Toll-free: 800-992-2908
Fax: 800-726-7112
www.fulcrumbooks.com